HIGHER ORDER THINKING SKILLS

Challenging ALL Students to Achieve

In A Nutshell
collection

R. Bruce Williams

CORWIN
A SAGE Company

For information:

Corwin
A SAGE Company
2455 Teller Road
Thousand Oaks,
    California 91320
(800) 233-9936
Fax: (800) 417-2466
www.corwinpress.com

SAGE Ltd.
1 Oliver's Yard
55 City Road
London EC1Y 1SP
United Kingdom

SAGE India Pvt. Ltd.
B 1/I 1 Mohan Cooperative
    Industrial Area
Mathura Road,
    New Delhi 110 044
India

SAGE Asia-Pacific Pte. Ltd.
33 Pekin Street #02-01
Far East Square
Singapore 048763

Printed in the United States of America

A catalog record of this book is available from the Library of Congress.

ISBN: 978-0-9717-3325-1

This book is printed on acid-free paper.

09   10   11   12   13   10   9   8   7   6   5   4   3   2   1

HIGHER ORDER THINKING SKILLS

In A Nutshell

s e r i e s

Dedication

To Jim Kelly who compassionately blends his heart with his profound thoughtfulness in order to bring life to those who he cares for.

■□■□■

Contents

■ □ ■ □ ■

INTRODUCTION

THE SITUATION NOW

As the stakes are raised in testing and accountability, recall of subject matter has become more and more important. However, both past and present voices are raising questions about using recall as the sole bottom line of schooling. Although recall is important, recall is not to be confused with depth knowledge, thought, and learning. As Paul said, "To this day we have refused to face these facts about knowledge, thought, and learning. To this day we commonly teach as if mere recall were equivalent to knowledge" (1993, p. viii).

There is no question that recall is crucial in this day of high-stakes testing. Furthermore, brain research is teaching educators about many ways to assist students in recalling information. However, recall alone is not enough for the person of the twenty-first century. Indeed, some standardized testing does reflect the demand for skills that go far beyond recall:

Recall alone is not enough for the person of the twenty-first century.

Yet classroom instruction around the world, at all levels, is typically didactic, one-dimensional, and indifferent, when not antithetical, to reason. Blank faces are taught barren conclusions in dreary drills. There is nothing sharp, nothing poignant, no exciting twist or turn of mind and thought, nothing fearless, nothing modest, no struggle, no conflict, no rational give-and-take, no intellectual excitement or discipline, no pulsation in the heart or mind. Students are not expected to ask for reasons to justify what they are told to believe. They do not question what they see, hear, or read, nor are they encouraged to do so. . . .They do not challenge the thinking of other students nor expect their thinking to be challenged by others. (Paul, 1993, p. ix)

Teachers cheat their students if all they ask of them is recall. By asking only for recall, teachers convey the message that the students' own thinking is not valuable and that questioning and challenging ideas is not welcome—this makes for very boring class situations and creates minds that are dull and lazy. Talk about "dumbing down" the curriculum.

THE CASE FOR HIGHER ORDER THINKING

As educators look ahead to future schools, much of the data and information they rely on today may be changed or repudiated. "To prepare our young people for the possibilities and probabilities of the future that few of us can imagine, the wisest course seems to be a curriculum that triggers their critical and creative thinking" (Bellanca & Fogarty, 1986, p. 5).

What can remain forever useful to the students of today is the capacity to think clearly and creatively in life and work situations. Prentice makes it clear: "Teaching thinking is an essential foundation for developing the minds of tomorrow's adults" (Prentice, 1994, p. xi). In addition to requiring crucial data, information, concepts, processes, and tools, teachers are being called on to enable the thinking of every student. To prepare students for the world of rapid change, it is absolutely imperative that teachers groom their students to think critically and to think on their own. Consequently, the role of higher order thinking, which has been encouraged by educators since the 1980s, has become more important than ever. Caine and Caine point this out:

It is absolutely imperative that teachers groom their students to think critically and to think on their own.

> Perhaps the most significant thing we have confirmed for ourselves is that, although actions are important, the thinking that influences and shapes what we do is far more critical. Changing our thinking is the first thing we have to do both individually and collectively, because without that change we cannot possibly change what we really do on a day-to-day basis. (1997, p. vi)

The ability to think critically that comes with having the tools for higher order thinking can help students far into their future not only grasp new information and material but also figure out how to change and adapt to new situations. Meir says, "Feuerstein argues that enhancing a child's cognitive abilities can have a snowballing effect in that, with these abilities enhanced, the child is capable of learning additional and even more complex cognitive operations and strategies" (Meir, 1994, p. 90). Feuerstein offers the possibility of ever-increasing higher order thinking capacities as more and more higher order thinking occurs. Earlier, Paul suggested that higher order thinking has a direct connection to the quality of life.

Elder and Paul strongly articulate that "thinking is at the heart of our future, not only for our society but for every society in the world" (1994, p. 34). They suggest three massive trends are gaining predominance: accelerating change, intensifying complexity, and increasing interdependence (p. 34). In their perspective, this makes it crystal clear that only minds that are adept at higher order thinking skills can deal with the change, the complexity, and the interdependence that now are inextricably part of the world.

THE HIGHER ORDER THINKING CLASSROOM OF THE FUTURE

What clues do educators have as to the nature of the higher order thinking classroom of the future? Sylwester (1995) envisions a classroom where teachers draw abilities out of a student as well as offer information to the student. He sees teachers helping students create their own framework of categories rather than being handed a framework from the teacher (p. 23). "It isn't enough for students to be in a stimulating environment—they have to help create it and directly interact with it. They have to have many opportunities to tell their stories, not just to listen to the teacher's stories" (p. 131).

Teachers have known for years that students rise to the expectations their teachers have of them. That is why Sylwester (1995) proposes that teachers not only provide students with a dynamic environment but also allow students to fashion that environment and be active within it. For students, he says, "Such activities as student projects, cooperative learning, and portfolio assessments place students at the center of the educative process, and thus stimulate learning" (p. 132). He also says, "Thus, teachers and parents become *facilitators*, who help to shape a stimulating social environment that helps students to work alone and together to solve the problems they confront" (p. 139).

All of this can promote an environment of higher order thinking given the skills of the teacher to ask higher order questions and pose appropriately complex problems to solve. As Sylwester says,

> Edelman's model of our brain as a rich, layered, messy, unplanned jungle ecosystem is especially intriguing, however, because it suggests that a junglelike brain might thrive best in a junglelike classroom that includes many sensory, cultural, and problem layers that are closely related to the real-world environment in which we live—the environment that best stimulates the neural networks that are genetically tuned to it. (Sylwester, 1995, p. 23)

Although the average teacher might be appalled at the notion of "a junglelike classroom," many insightful teachers yearn for a rich, complex classroom that challenges the senses, emotions, and thinking of all the students. It is this very "junglelike classroom" that can allow buried gifts and strengths in the student to come to the fore. It is such a "junglelike classroom" that could call forth higher order thinking from every student.

Many insightful teachers yearn for a rich, complex classroom that challenges the senses, emotions, and thinking of all the students.

The higher order thinking classroom of the future "is a classroom in which the teacher purposefully gives priority to teaching students multiple ways to think about what they are learning" (Bellanca & Fogarty, 1986, p. 4). This may seem obvious to teachers, yet so many teachers are constrained by demands to produce higher test scores or to inculcate the state or district standards that delving into the teaching of thinking seems impossible in an already crowded lesson. This is in spite of the fact that essentially educators have known how to do this for some time: "We have made giant strides in identifying ways to improve instruction so that all students can learn faster and better. Included in these improvements are the methodologies to help all students become more skillful thinkers" (Bellanca & Fogarty, 1986, p. 3).

Another crucial concern is helping all teachers believe that all students *can* think. Again, this is a critical expectation for teachers to bring to the classroom. When a teacher has decided that only one-third of a particular class can think, then his or her instruction is vastly different than when he or she presumes that, on some level, all students are able to think:

> If and when teachers believe that all students *can* think. . .and all students *need* to think, that message is communicated to the students. Teachers who value thinking challenge all students to stretch. These teachers cause students to interpret, analyze, translate, hypothesize, predict, apply, synthesize, and evaluate what they learn. They expect students to discuss, debate, answer high level questions, prove, write, think aloud and critically and creatively attach the ideas shared by the teacher, the texts and peers. (Bellanca & Fogarty, 1986, p. 6)

Needless to say, higher order thinking as described by Bellanca and Fogarty does not happen overnight. It takes time and effort, and thus, may seem overwhelming to teachers with already crowded schedules. But, effort in the area of higher order thinking certainly pays off in the long run—even on the unavoidable standardized tests. The most difficult step may be changing one's belief from only *some* children are able to think in a higher level to *all* children are able to think in a higher level. "Starting with the belief that all children can learn to think more critically and creatively, the effective teacher need do little more than add to her repertoire of skills and methodologies that promote skillful thinking" (Bellanca & Fogarty, 1986, p. 6).

> **Effort in the area of higher order thinking certainly pays off in the long run.**

The Five Rs

Higher order thinking categories were suggested first by William E. Doll, Jr. in an 1993 article called "Curriculum Possibilities in a 'Post'-Future." He used four categories to illuminate future curriculum: Richness, Recursion, Relations, and Rigor. Fogarty (1997) built on Doll's categories and articulated a modified five categories: Relevance, Richness, Relatedness, Rigor, and Recursiveness (see Figure Intro. 1). These five categories, called the Five Rs, clarify why higher order thinking skills are urgently needed for every student.

■□■□■

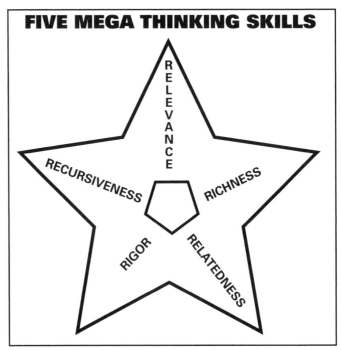

Figure Intro.1. Five mega thinking skills.

THE LIFE QUESTIONS

Most educators understand that higher order thinking, although abstract, is necessary for students in classrooms. However, it is equally important to understand that higher order thinking is necessary for students outside classrooms as well. Higher order thinking skills are not just important for getting through school (which goal for some students generates a "So what?" attitude) but also are critical for getting through life. With thoughtful work by teachers to relate

Higher order thinking skills are not just important for getting through school but also are critical for getting through life.

higher order thinking skills to everyday life needs and to each human's life questions, the relevancy of higher order thinking skills to life does not go unnoticed. Unless this connection is made and perhaps even overemphasized, students may not understand the need for such skills.

Consequently, as part of the discussion of each of the five Rs, some of the appropriate life questions are identified and discussed. Of course, there may be different ones for different students at different times and in different situations.

THREE LEVELS

Late in the 1980s, Fogarty and Bellanca articulated three levels of thinking in a construct they called the "Three Story Intellect" (Fogarty & Bellanca, 1991, p. 89). They called these three levels gathering, processing, and applying. In the first-story gathering level, teachers enable students to get acquainted with data, information, and concepts. Teachers check this level of understanding by asking questions using verbs such as *describe, recite, tell, name*, and so on. In the second-story processing level, teachers encourage students to work with the data, information, and concepts to move toward deep understanding of the material. It is in this level that the meaning and significance of the material becomes clear. Teachers check this level of understanding by asking questions using verbs such as *compare and contrast, explain why, analyze, categorize, infer*, and so forth. In the third-story applying level, teachers emphasize the usefulness and applicability of the material to everyday life. Teachers check this level of understanding by asking questions using verbs such as *imagine, predict, create, evaluate, speculate*, and so on.

■□■□■

Patterned after the construct of the three levels of thinking, higher order thinking skills also have been arranged in three levels: understanding information, generating insight, and discerning implications. Let's look at each more closely.

Understanding Information

The first level in higher order thinking skills, *understanding information*, starts one level up from Fogarty and Bellanca's first-story gathering level. Merely repeating data and information or merely recalling and reciting are not really activities of higher order thinking. Fogarty and Bellanca's first level is not treated in this book.

Learners move into higher order thinking when they wrestle with the data and information in order to make some sense of it, when they compare and contrast, when they attempt to explain why, or when they categorize data and information. This level, which starts with Fogarty and Bellanca's second-story processing level, begins this book.

Generating Insight

The next, deeper step in higher order thinking is called *generating insight*. There comes a time when learners have so adequately processed and so deeply grasped information that they are able to build their own insights directly related to the data. At this point, learners are generating ideas about the data and information that indicate that genuine understanding has been gained. In addition, learners may be taking the data and information one step further with such insights. At this time, perhaps the "Aha!" happens.

Discerning Implications

The final level is *discerning implications*. There is a time when the implications of the data and information become clear. That is, a learner begins to act, create, predict, judge, and evaluate the data and information. This is most akin to the third-story applying level suggested by Fogarty and Bellanca. Some teachers suggest that it is only at this stage that data and information really become a part of students' minds. Other teachers suggest that only now can students start having fun with the data and information that they have so laboriously comprehended. It is at this point that the real relevancy of data and information becomes clear and that students see connections between data and information and real life.

Figure Intro.2 shows fifteen higher order thinking strategies arranged by category and by thinking level. This figure is meant to be a brief overview; each strategy is examined in the chapter that discusses its category and thinking level.

A MATRIX OF HIGHER ORDER THINKING SKILLS

© R. BRUCE WILLIAMS

Toward Deep Comprehension	Relevance-Contemporaneity	Richness-Complexity	Relatedness-Connetedness	Rigor-Challenge	Recursiveness-Concept
Understanding Information	Comparing/ Contrasting	Classifying/ Sorting/ Ranking	Connecting	Explaining Why	Analyzing
Generating Insights	Evaluating/ Judging	Visualizing/ Imagining	Forcing Relationships	Inferring	Making Analogies
Discerning Implications	Applying	Creating/ Innovating/ Inventing	Generalizing	Sequencing/ Predicting	Transferring

Figure Intro.2. Higher order thinking skills matrix.

Strategy Techniques

Within each of the fifteen sections devoted to the specific thinking skills, two crucial teaching techniques are emphasized. One technique is to ask specific kinds of questions to help students become familiar with and strengthen that particular thinking skill. Posing these questions helps to guide students into recognizing and using a thinking skill.

The second technique is a graphic organizer that helps students to visualize how to use that particular thinking skill. By making a thinking skill visible in a graphic organizer, teachers enable students who do not automatically understand thinking skills to grasp their power. Teachers well versed in higher order questioning and adept at these and other graphic organizers consistently will raise the level of higher order thinking skills in their classrooms.

Many students find pictorial ways of organizing information extremely helpful in understanding and remembering content material. The graphic organizers shown in Figure Intro.3 are especially helpful as products for cooperative teams. Furthermore, when teachers want to emphasize a particular thinking skill, such as comparing and contrasting, analyzing, or sequencing, the graphic organizer linked with that thinking skill may be appropriate for their lesson. At least one graphic organizer is shown for each of the fifteen thinking skill areas outlined in this book.

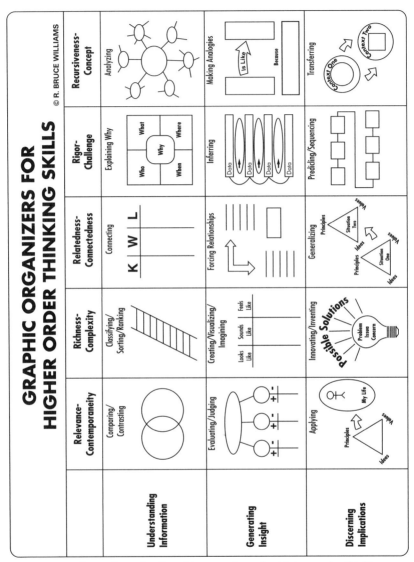

Figure Intro.3. Graphic organizers for higher order thinking skills.

About This Book

I invite you to peruse this book in any way you choose. You may like to start here and read to the finish. Or, you may want to target a particularly intriguing category and dig in there. This book is offered in the hopes that higher order thinking skills will continue to blossom even more dramatically in our classrooms of the twenty-first century.

Each chapter treats one category of thinking skills. A chapter begins with a brief anecdote that illustrates the category, then discusses the skill, presents relevant life questions, and concludes by examining chosen strategies for the three thinking levels. Appendix A presents a brainstorming and lesson planning approach; Appendix B includes a blank copy of each of the graphic organizers presented in the text.

■ □ ■ □ ■

RELEVANCE

I was visiting my son and grandson near Philadelphia on a weekend before I had a workshop presentation in New Jersey. All three of us enjoyed a good time together. On our way to have Sunday brunch, my then five-year-old grandson asked, "Why do you have to go?" I replied, "I have work to do with 25 teachers over in New Jersey." Very quickly he responded, "Then have them all come over here so you can stay." My grandson's higher order thinking took me aback. He had processed the information and come up with a very logical solution that honored my need to work with the teachers and his desire to have me stay longer. His higher order thinking was definitely focused on relevance for himself. Relevance, in other words, was the spark for his leap in higher order thinking.

About Relevance

There are three criteria that can help teachers gauge whether something is relevant to a student's thinking and to a student's life. First, can the situation, material, or learning connect with a student's emotions? Second, can the situation, material, or learning reveal some meaning or significance to the student? And, third, can the situation, material, or learning help to bring the student to a state of flow (Csikszentmihalyi, 1990)? These three doorways—emotions, significance, and flow—can help students see that something is relevant to them and thereby prompt higher order thinking.

■ □ ■ □ ■

THE ROLE OF EMOTIONS

Cognitive science has tried to understand higher order thinking in many different ways. It has focused on cognitive processes as devoid of emotion (LeDoux, 1996, p. 25). Many philosophers and contemporary psychologists have worked hard at distinguishing thinking and feeling, seeing them as very separate functions in the human mind (LeDoux, 1996, p. 35). However, as Goleman reports:

> Because so many of the brain's higher centers sprouted from or extended the scope of the limbic area, the emotional brain plays a crucial role in neural architecture. As the root from which the newer brain grew, the emotional areas are intertwined via myriad connecting circuits to all parts of the neocortex. This gives the emotional centers immense power to influence the functioning of the rest of the brain—including its centers for thought. (1995, p. 12)

Goleman makes it clear that there are many connections between emotion and thinking. Consequently, attempts at creating relevance that exclude emotion will have a very difficult task energizing higher order thinking.

It stands to reason that appropriate involvement of emotion in the learning environment can enhance higher order thinking. Sylwester furthers this line of thinking by suggesting that "We know emotion is very important to the educative process because it drives attention, which drives learning and memory" (1995, p. 72). In other words, emotions can be the very gateway to attention, which, in turn, becomes the gateway to learning and memory. The same can be said relative to higher order thinking. Emotions are the gateway to attention, and attention, then, is the gateway to higher order thinking. "All point to a simple truth: if one wants something to be attended to, mastered, and subsequently used, one must be sure to wrap it in a context that engages the emotions" (Gardner, 2000, p. 77).

> **Emotions are the gateway to attention, and attention, then, is the gateway to higher order thinking.**

Although the effect of emotions on thinking has been emphasized, Elder and Paul complete the circle by suggesting that higher order thinking can alter feelings. They say, "We must recognize that feelings are products of thinking, and that it is only through thinking that feelings become altered" (1997, p. 41). This research says that emotions are deeply interconnected to students' higher order thinking and, furthermore, enable them to see the relevance in content material and, thus, enter into higher order thinking.

THE IMPORTANCE OF MEANING

"Deep meaning refers to whatever drives us and governs our sense of purpose" (Caine & Caine, 1997, p. 111). Therefore, another entry point into relevance is meaning. If the student cannot discern any meaning in the situation, material, or learning, then the student will not be motivated to think.

Caine and Caine also point out that our brains are constructed to "make sense of life experience" (1997, p. 118). The more teachers enable the brains of their students to find patterns and to make sense, the more they are facilitating their students ability to discern the relevance

■ □ ■ □ ■

in situations, materials, and learning. Caine and Caine devoted two of their brain/mind learning principles to the importance of meaning: "Principle 3: The search for meaning is innate," and "Principle 4: The search for meaning occurs through 'patterning'" (1997, p. 19). They proposed that the brain is a meaning-creating organ. Creating meaning is one of its jobs. Students' thinking is intensified when they use their brains to create their own meaning out of material they have been given or have found. Thinking and memories are intensified when students have invested personal meaning in them (Sylwester, 1995, p. 96). Caine and Caine note that when content material comes alive for a student— called dynamical knowledge by them—that "Dynamical knowledge is what we end up with as a result of our constructing our own meanings" (1997, p. 114). Consequently, meaning becomes crucial for generating a sense of relevance. That is, meaning becomes one pathway into higher order thinking.

> Students' thinking is intensified when they use their brains to create their own meaning out of material they have been given or have found.

THE IMPACT OF FLOW

Csikszentmihalyi (1990) introduced the concept of flow to describe a pleasing state of involvement relative to learning or working on a project or participating in a hobby. "When a learner experiences a state of flow, a creative oasis is reached, and the performer takes great pleasure in encountering the complexities of the task. The performer is free of frustration, fatigue, and futility. In fact, the performer has this feeling of intense enjoyment and joy in the performance of the skill" (Fogarty, 1997, p. 131). When in this state, the person feels a passion for learning more or practicing a particular skill more completely. In fact, there is no stopping the student's capacity to absorb content material related to the topic that has captured his or her attention. Thought and feeling are merged at this point.

"Being able to enter flow is emotional intelligence at its best; flow represents perhaps the ultimate in harnessing the emotions in the service of performance and learning. In flow the emotions are not just contained and channeled, but positive, energized, and aligned with the task at hand" (Goleman, 1995, p. 90). The tricky task for the teacher is to present a task with just the right amount of challenge so that the student has the possibility of entering flow. "If a task is too simple, it is boring; if too challenging, the result is anxiety rather than flow" (Goleman, 1995, p. 93).

One of Caine and Caine's principles is that "complex learning is enhanced by challenge and inhibited by threat" (1997, p. 19). Although clearly the emotional state of the student has a direct impact on the possibility of flow, genuine flow is an optimum mixture of emotions and meaning. In other words, when an arena both beckons emotional involvement from and reveals a great deal of deep meaning for the student, then that student has the possibility of entering into the state of flow and engaging in thought-filled learning. Figure 1.1 shows this mix, which gives educators clues as to the potential for relevance as one facet leading to higher order thinking.

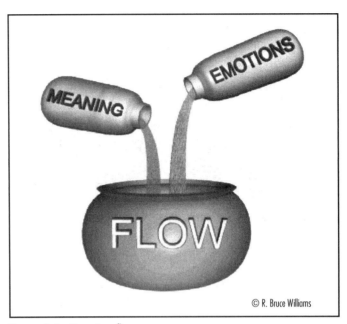

© R. Bruce Williams

Figure 1.1. Creating flow.

THE LIFE QUESTION

The concept of relevancy poses this life question for students: How do I make sense of who I am?

As learning directly connects a student with this life question, that student has the possibility of moving into higher order thinking. If students do not see how higher order thinking can help them make sense of who they are, then they are not motivated to stretch into higher order thinking. This means that teachers need to be not only competent in the particular content area but also deeply aware of the life situations and complexities of the lives of their students.

Understanding Information—Skills of Comparing and Contrasting

Description of Strategy

Comparing and contrasting are two thinking skills that help students grasp whether information is relevant. How is this information linked with what they already understand? How is this information different from what they have been thinking or from what they have learned before? Comparing and contrasting take the ability to discern what the characteristics are of what is already known and what the characteristics are of what is being presented and to recognize their similarities or differences. It is these skills that enable a person to see connections between literary characters and the person's own characteristics and struggles or to decide which candidate to vote for in an election.

Comparing and contrasting are two thinking skills that help students grasp whether information is relevant.

Although this skill is vital to learning content material in school, it is also vital to the person walking down the street and noticing a gathering of people ahead. What does this person know already about benign gatherings of people? What does this person know already about the signs of danger in gatherings of people? How does that compare and/or contrast with what is just up ahead? The accuracy of the walker's higher order thinking can make the difference between walking straight ahead into the group or crossing the street and avoiding the group altogether. In some cases, these skills can make the difference between safety and danger, even life and death

Link to Relevance

In actuality, students are often comparing and contrasting. One reason that many students drop out of school is that they take information given to them in school and contrast that with their daily lives. When the contrast reveals no relevance to their daily lives, they discard the information. The challenge for teachers is to demonstrate how comparing and contrasting of content material can lead to a sense of deep relevance for the student.

Teaching Hints

Very often, the clue to linking data and information or stories to a student is through concepts and themes. A story written by Shakespeare reveals themes that every human struggles with. Getting too buried in the older English language, getting too overwhelmed with remembering what happened first and what happened next, or getting too pressured to recall myriads of characters may deter the student from seeing the real relevancy of the material. That is why using comparing and contrasting skills to reveal concepts, struggles, and themes that the student is currently experiencing can be the gateway to seeing the power of whatever content is being taught.

Questions

Comparing and contrasting are foundational skills for students. To help students discover links and differences, consider asking these kinds of questions:

How are two people alike and how are they different?

How is this character in the novel like you and how is he or she different?

How are you like this historical figure and how are you different?

How is this historical event like what just happened in x place yesterday?

How does this piece of information connect or disconnect with what you studied last week?

How is what you would do similar to or dissimilar to what this historical figure did?

Now that you have read these two novels or stories, why does one have more relevance to your life than the other?

The Graphic Organizer

The most popular graphic organizer to use for comparing and contrasting is a Venn diagram—two circles that overlap (Figure 1.2). In one circle, list the characteristics of the first item. In the other circle, list the characteristics of the second item. In the overlapping section, list common characteristics that each item has.

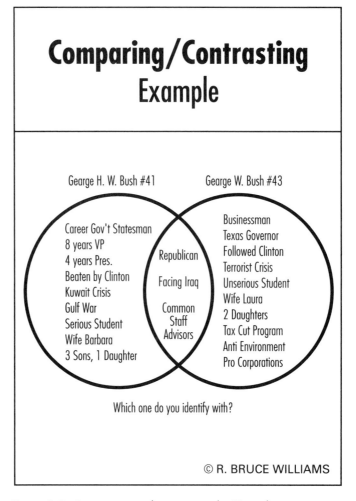

Figure 1.2. Comparing and contrasting by Venn diagram example.

Some teachers have created a Y figure (Figure 1.3), with the two contrasting characteristics above the Y and the common characteristics below the Y.

Comparing/Contrasting
Example

Bill Clinton	George W. Bush #43
Rhodes Scholar	Businessman
Lawyer	Texas Governor
Arkansas Governor	Followed Clinton
Followed Gearge H W Bush	Terrorist Crisis
Pro-Environment	Unserious Student
Waco TX Crisis	Wife Laura
Oklahoma City Bombing	2 Daughters
Focus on Economy	Tax Cut Program
Impeachment	Anti Environment
Sex Scandals	Pro Corporations
Reduced Deficit	

Y

Southern Governors
Baby Boomers
Daughters
Rallied Public Support

Which one do you identify with?

© R. BRUCE WILLIAMS

Figure 1.3. Comparing and contrasting using a Y example.

Generating Insight—Skills of Evaluating and Judging

Description of Strategy

Two thinking skills that help students in processing relevance are evaluating and judging. It is at this point that students insert their opinions and values into the data and information that they are working with. Having grasped some of the meaning of the information and using their personal thoughts, contexts, and values, students come up with very individual and personal insights. There is a weighing process that assumes a rich dialogue going on in the minds and hearts of students as they make personal decisions and judgments. In other words, this is not a process of taking data and information at face value but rather a process of examining behind, above, below, in between, and along side of the data and information and then connecting that examination not only with previous information but also with ongoing principles, values, and personal thoughts and opinions.

Link to Relevance

Merely understanding information is not enough to foster relevancy. Students need the skill of evaluating and judging to really determine whether there is meaning in the material for them personally. This demands getting intimate with the material—mixing one's own viewpoint, concerns, and desires with the material—to the point that understanding turns to grasping significance and meaning for one's own life.

Teaching Hints

Teachers cannot assume that their students, no matter what age level, come to them with developed thinking skills. Consequently, teachers need to teach thinking skills very directly and explicitly (Fogarty & Opeka, 1988, p. i). Teachers need to break down the process of evaluating and judging so that they create a road map to successful evaluations and judgments for their students.

> **Teachers need to teach thinking skills very directly and explicitly (Fogarty & Opeka, 1988, p. i).**

Questions

Evaluating and judging are student activities whether done properly or not. To help students develop correct and useful ways to weigh things, people, and situations, consider asking students questions like this:

Which alternative makes more sense to you? Why does it make more sense to you?

Which approach will reach the most ethical resolution of this issue? Why?

What are the relevant values to keep in mind in order to settle this issue?

What are the consequences of doing x or doing y?

What are the relevant perspectives getting revealed?

What criteria are you using to make your judgments?

Graphic Organizer

Evaluating and judging have something to do with making a decision about options or getting clarity on the strengths and weaknesses or advantages and disadvantages of something. The graphic organizer shown in Figure 1.4 helps students either to examine a topic or situation in detail and see clearly the positives and negatives or to grasp the positives and negatives in two or more options. The ellipse on top of the options is a place to put the results of this evaluation and judgment. It is entirely possible that the contents of the ellipse could be a combination of elements in the two or three options.

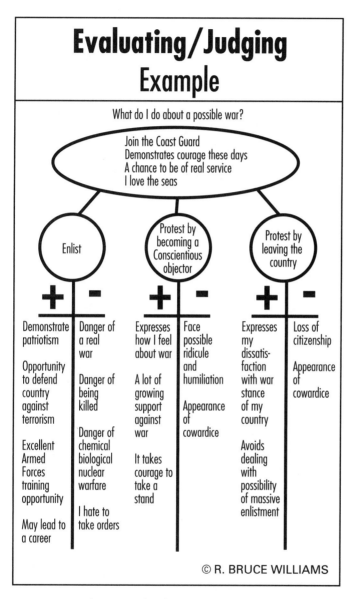

Evaluating/Judging
Example

What do I do about a possible war?

Join the Coast Guard
Demonstrates courage these days
A chance to be of real service
I love the seas

Enlist

Protest by becoming a Conscientious objector

Protest by leaving the country

+	−	+	−	+	−
Demonstrate patriotism	Danger of a real war	Expresses how I feel about war	Face possible ridicule and humiliation	Expresses my dissatis-faction with war stance of my country	Loss of citizenship
Opportunity to defend country against terrorism	Danger of being killed	A lot of growing support against war	Appearance of cowardice		Appearance of cowardice
Excellent Armed Forces training opportunity	Danger of chemical biological nuclear warfare	It takes courage to take a stand		Avoids dealing with possibility of massive enlistment	
May lead to a career	I hate to take orders				

© R. BRUCE WILLIAMS

Figure 1.4. Evaluating and judging example.

In addition to the graphic in Figure 1.4, a second visual representation that teachers could make of the process of evaluating and judging is to illuminate the steps that students already use when they make personal evaluations and judgments (for they are making those every day about many choices in their lives) by listing the steps on an overhead or a wall board.

Discerning Implications— Skill of Applying

Description of Strategy

When students have adequately understood information and have begun to spin off insights from that information, they are ready to apply the information to their own lives. Applying information involves the students' ability to pull out concepts, principles, ideas, and values and connect them to everyday life. This also requires that students have some ability to examine their own lives. In other words, applying information calls for a capacity to step back from the material and information to see what is valuable in it and to step back from everyday life enough to see its applicability. To do this, students need some grasp of where they are heading and what their particular needs are to get there. Students immersed in immediacy and the short term may have great difficulty in doing this. In other words, the skill of pulling principles, ideas, and values out of information is only half of the skill necessary for application. The other part of the skill is the ability to analyze and grasp what is going on in one's own life. Without students' ability to relate information to their own lives, teachers have plugs without sockets, so to speak.

Link to Relevance

The skill of applying is the crucial skill that finally makes material meaningful to students' everyday lives. Without this step, material may be interesting and intriguing, but not necessarily relevant. Many teachers observe that without this skill of applying, the material never really becomes permanently the student's own. Other teachers observe that this is when the learning has become fun. Without applying, there can be no impacting relevancy.

> **Without applying, there can be no impacting relevancy.**

Teaching Hints

Applying is one of the hardest thinking skills to use. In general, students do not see connections between material studied and their own lives. Because of this, teachers need to present the steps of applying in order, thus helping students move, step-by-step, toward full applying. This is why it is so crucial to encourage students to articulate whatever perspectives, principles, or deep beliefs they hold. Getting students to articulate their real questions about life can lead them to discover relevant principles, values, and ideas in the material they are working with. Some students may need one-on-one work here. Other students will be able to do this introspection on their own or in the context of small group work.

Questions

Applying questions are particularly important to help students relate school content to their lives. Questions that foster application include these:

> When have you encountered this issue in your own life?
>
> When have you lost something dear to you?
>
> How might you use this outside of this classroom?
>
> What opportunities and challenges does this situation present?
>
> Does might this approach really challenge or call into question how you have handled things so far? How?
>
> What new direction is this calling you to consider?

Graphic Organizer

The graphic organizer shown in Figure 1.5 is particularly useful in helping students apply what they are learning to their personal lives. Students look at the data and concepts, pull out any principles, values, or ideas, and try to see any relevance among any of them to their own lives. One aid to students in doing this is for them to figure out what their own principles, values, beliefs, and life questions are. Many times, connection are not made because students are not really clear about where they are coming from or what personal goals they have.

Figure 1.5. Applying example.

RICHNESS

I went to high school and college on the East coast. My peers and friends came from many different backgrounds: Catholic, Protestant, Jewish, Asian, Hispanic, and African-American. Following college, I taught in a junior college on the island of Okinawa, and became immersed in a different culture, a different language, and different religious perspectives. I relished the chance to experience all this difference.

On my return to the United States, I entered graduate school in the Midwest. Whenever I talked positively about my overseas experience, I was met with "If you liked it so much, why don't you just go back?" What was exciting and thought-provoking for me was offensive and devaluing to my peers and friends in graduate school. To this day, I am grateful for the richness that expanded my higher order thinking. Maybe all this enabled me, years later, to adopt as my own children a brother and a sister from Korea.

About Richness

What does it mean to say that richness is one of the facets of higher order thinking? What does it mean to say that higher order thinking grants one a special richness? To begin with, richness implies diversity, a multitude of perspectives, and a broad scope or view of things. Another facet of richness is articulated by Gardner with three words: the true, the beautiful, and the good (2000, p. 16). Richness leads into the arena of all the arts. Finally, richness points to character, morality, and values. The richness aspect of higher order thinking gives to students an overflowing smorgasbord of rich variety rather than a fast food sandwich of low-level thinking. In other words, higher order thinking is crucial in allowing a person to experience the richness of life.

THE WEALTH OF DIVERSITY

It is not easy to live in a world that is undergoing a shift from relative homogeneity to great diversity. Many schools today are participating in that shift. "We now live in a global village, with rapid change and constant contact with thousands of others. The more experiences we have, the more media we are exposed to, the more people we interact with, the greater the differences that are likely to emerge. Diversity is the order of the millennium" (Gardner, 1999, p. 217).

The more teachers encourage the development of thought-filled diversity and the more they expose the diversity inherent in their schools, the more they are preparing their students to live in the real world. As teachers honor appropriately the diversity that is already present, they challenge their students into higher order thinking. Gardner shares a very personal, dynamic hope for the future: "I envision a world citizenry that is highly literate, disciplined, capable of thinking critically and creatively, knowledgeable about a range of cultures, able to participate in discussion about new discoveries and choices, willing to take risks for what it believes in" (Gardner, 2000, p. 25).

One obvious implication of richness is that teachers have a broader appreciation of the differences students bring into their classrooms. When educators take seriously the fact that one size does not fit all, there are radical implications for what, how, and why they teach (Gardner, 1999, p. 91). Do teachers convey the content material in a variety of instructional strategies to speak to the diverse ways of learning among their students? Do teachers challenge all of their students to represent their knowledge in more than one way so that they can be sure that their students really understand the material and are not just parroting memorized material? (Gardner, 1999, p. 178) When honored appropriately, diversity can challenge each individual's thinking, thus clarifying and transforming the thinking of each student.

> **When honored appropriately, diversity can challenge each individual's thinking.**

THE POWER OF THE TRUE, THE BEAUTIFUL, AND THE GOOD

In some ways, the mushrooming of diversity and globalization has steered education away from concerns of what is really true, beautiful, and good. In this era of challenge and confusion, society has demanded that education steer clear of such controversial arenas. However, Gardner insists "education must *continue* to confront truth (falsity), beauty (ugliness), and goodness (evil), in full awareness of the problematic facets of these categories and the disagreements across cultures and subcultures" (2000, p. 35).

Gardner's assertion is pointing to exactly why diversity is coming up in higher order thinking skills. Rather than providing lockstep answers to these crucial life questions and societal concerns, educators should pose the appropriate questions to enable students to discover their own answers. Teachers need to help students develop their higher order thinking so that it is the students who may discern the consequences and visualize the possibilities of certain choices about what is true, beautiful, and good. Robbing education of dialogue around these three qualities paves the way to a culture bereft of thought-filled conceptions of the true, beautiful, and good. To put it bluntly, "No culture can endure unless it attains some success in passing on its chosen verities, beauties, and desired modes of behavior" (Gardner, 2000, p. 212). This is why the promotion of the arts in schools is so vital. It is in the midst of participation in art, music, drama, and sculpture that one has to make decisions about truth, beauty, and goodness.

> **Educators should pose the appropriate questions to enable students to discover their own answers.**

THE DEPTH OF CHARACTER, MORALITY, AND VALUES

A related arena is the third aspect of richness—character, morality, and values. This aspect involves the role of higher order thinking in helping to develop solid character and ethical values. Character and ethics are not developed by reading books or by memorizing a code of ethics. The issues confronting men and women in the twenty-first century are more complex and more demanding than ever before. As Gardner says, ". . . literacies, skills, and disciplines ought to be pursued as tools that allow us to enhance our understanding of important questions, topics, and themes" (1999, p. 159). Schools can become the safe arena in which controversial perspectives and values are examined critically so that students can develop the ability to decide those issues that will be thrust on them sooner rather than later. Without an intense emphasis on higher order thinking skills, students will not have developed the tools to make thoughtful choices nor will they have the motivation to develop depth of character. Again, Gardner illuminates the issue:

> But the task for the new millennium is not merely to hone our various intelligences and use them properly. We must figure out how intelligence and morality can work together to create a world in which a great variety of people will want to live. . . . Intelligence is valuable, but, as Ralph Waldo Emerson famously remarked, "Character is more important than intellect." That insight applies at both the individual and the societal levels. (1999, p. 4)

THE LIFE QUESTIONS

The life questions posed by the arena of richness include:

How does my life become worthwhile?

How does my life become fulfilled?

How does my life make a difference?

How will whatever we are working on enhance the quality of my life?

Although profound, these questions may seem impossible to pose to students who are swept into the concern of the moment and the passions of growing into adults. Yet, the implications to students and adults of ignoring these particular life questions are manifested in violent and destructive acts. Finding the pathway that allows educators to raise these questions of richness can also give them the pathway to encouraging higher order thinking skills.

Understanding Information—Skills of Classifying, Sorting, and Ranking

Description of Strategy

Students use classifying, sorting, and ranking skills to work with information—to organize it, to categorize it, to make priority judgments about it—in order to understand what the data are about and what is being conveyed. *Classifying* refers to naming the clusters into which data can be organized. *Sorting* refers to clustering data and information with other pieces of related data and information. *Ranking* refers to giving data or clusters a priority—that is, this is most important; this is fairly important; this is the least important of these data or of these clusters. Classifying, sorting, and ranking are ways to make sense out of information presented.

Link to Richness

Classifying, sorting, and ranking help students to begin to see the spectrum of material being studied. The acts of classifying, sorting, and ranking begin to reveal a big picture to students. Seeing the big picture is one road to perceiving the richness in the material and helps students raise questions about the value and the worth of the material. Classifying, sorting, and ranking actually assist the students' thinking and help them begin to grasp the depth and breadth of the material they are trying to learn. Through these thinking skills, students can begin to ask their own questions of the material.

Teaching Hints

Human brains have great difficulty remembering unrelated stacks of information because unrelated stacks of information do not communicate a reason to be remembered. The energy used to classify, sort, and rank is energy put into discovering the significance of the material and, thus, into learning and remembering the information. Teachers have to help students spend this energy in order to tap into the richness of the material.

Questions

Tasks that ask students to separate, group, and name are particularly useful for developing classification skills. Questions that foster classifying, sorting, and ranking tasks include the following:

> Into what five or six clusters could you organize these facts and data?

> What could you name these five or six different clusters?

How would you differentiate among them in order to perceive each cluster's uniqueness?

Which pairs of clusters are linked in some way?

Relative to this issue, how could you rank these clusters according to levels of impact or importance?

Graphic Organizer

The matrix (Figure 2.1) is a most helpful tool for classifying and sorting material. When two or three data are in a column, a title may be suggested. Gradually, as more and more clusters are discerned, the titles can be sharpened and clarified. It may even be possible to cut across categories and create a double matrix, with categories in rows as well as columns. This makes the matrix even more powerful when it can be done naturally. When the matrix is completed, it reveals relationships among the information that aid students' learning and memory processes. The matrix proclaims the richness and diversity of the material and helps to intrigue students with the material.

It is especially helpful to demonstrate a matrix several times for the whole class before asking individuals or teams to create one. In fact, laying out some simple steps could help guide students as they attempt to create a matrix on their own. Monitoring how individuals or teams have organized data is crucial to grasping how well they understand the material. On the other hand, creative organization of material often reveals some exciting thought processes on the part of the students.

Classifying/Sorting/Ranking
Example

	West	Midwest	South	North-east
Geographic	Mountains Desert Pacific Coast	Great Lakes Plains	Atlantic Shore Gulf Mississippi Delta	Atlantic Shore Appalachian Mountains
Economic	Technology Logging Fishing	Farming Industry Auto Industry	Fruit & Nut Farming Tourism	Technology Old Industry Fishing
Known for	National Praks Hollywood Grand Canyon	Chicago Land of Lincoln Bread basket	Hurricanes Tornadoes Gardens Confederate History	Early Colonial & Nation's History New York — Financial Ctr. Washington DC

© R. BRUCE WILLIAMS

Figure 2.1. Classifying, sorting, and ranking example.

For ranking information or concepts, the graphic organizer called the ranking ladder (Figure 2.2) can assist. The student writes the most important item in the first space in the ladder and continues with the next important, and then repeats the step until all items are covered. In the presentation of the ranking ladder, the student can add the values that were used in the prioritizing.

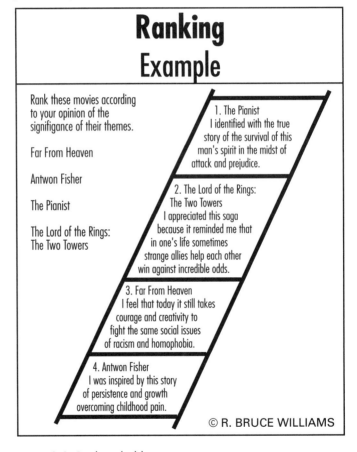

Figure 2.2. Ranking ladder.

Generating Insight—Skill of Visualizing and Imagining

Description of Strategy

Visualizing enables a person to actually see in his or her mind something being described. *Imagining* allows a person to put something totally new together in the mind. Both visualizing and imagining produce very concrete pictures in the mind. Both end up with something being pictured in the mind that has never before been seen with the eye. Whether it is a concept just learned or a description just read, visualizers see a clear picture of this in their minds. The imaginer may use some known material, but goes one step further and pictures something entirely new. By doing this, visualizers and imaginers demonstrate having absorbed, worked with, and then translated information from the verbal to the visual or pieced information together in a completely new way. This new way demonstrates the student's own insights generated out of the material given.

Link to Richness

The generating insight level of visualizing and imagining displays richness in higher order thinking by taking words and abstract concepts and making them real. This level further displays richness by going beyond what is given and coming up with a new picture. This level or interaction takes rich, complex ideas and makes them practical, real, and visible. It helps to reveal the richness in what only seems

> **Visualizing and imagining display richness in higher order thinking by taking words and abstract concepts and making them real.**

to be abstract and unrealizable. When others see this, they are often inspired to acts and feats thought impossible.

Teaching Hints

The thinking skills of visualizing and imagining will be exceedingly difficult for some students. Yet, encouraging these skills can prove rewarding for real learning in the classroom. Try pairing very visual with less visual students to increase the skill of visualizing among the students. Have a lot of visually stimulating material in the classroom to encourage students to become better at visualizing and imagining. Visualizing and imagining can make material come alive and deepen the higher order thinking process.

Questions

To encourage visualizing and imagining, ask questions or give prompts that engage students' visual skills. Questions or prompts to ask to foster visualizing and imagining include the following:

> If this character had chosen another path, what do you think would have happened?

> (Midway in a story), now write your own ending, given where the plot has led us this far.

> Draw a picture that communicates JUSTICE or FREEDOM or DIVERSITY.

> How would life in the United States be different if the South had won the Civil War?

■ ☐ ■ ☐ ■

Imagine how Al Gore would have responded to the events of 9/11.

What will your life look like 10 years from now?

Graphic Organizer

One graphic organizer that works well with the thinking skills of visualizing and imagining is the double t-chart (Figure 2.3) with the categories of Looks Like, Sounds Like, and Feels Like. In other words, take an abstract category, such as the American colonial period, and ask, "What does that look like, sound like, feel like?" Or, "What did slavery look like, sound like, feel like?" Or, "What does team work look like, sound like, feel like?" Some teachers have used the double t-chart to teach social skills. Others use the double t-chart to assist the visual and auditory learning styles.

Visualizing/Imagining
Example

Colonial Period of History

Looks Like	Sounds Like	Feels Like
Colonial Style Dress Houses	Chopping wood	Free from European persecution
Mother teaching children A, B, C's	Building homes	Daily challenges to survive
Men working to get food or cash	Sunday services	
	Dissatisfaction with connections to England & France	

© R. BRUCE WILLIAMS

Figure 2.3. Visualizing and imagining example.

Discerning Implications—Skills of Creating, Innovating, and Inventing

Description of Strategy

The thinking skills of creating, innovating, and inventing build on the complexity of material students have studied and enable the student to come up with something that no one has thought of in quite that way before. *Creating* seems particularly applicable in the area of the arts. After learning about form, clay, perspective, and texture, a student creates a piece of sculpture that is unique and new. After learning about syntax, story forms, and spelling, one writes an original story. After learning about music theory, studying various instruments, and analyzing the music of different composers, one creates an original piece of music.

Innovating comes from discerning a particular need and figuring out a way to meet that need with something that has been used before.

Inventing comes into play when the usual way of doing something does not work any more. One is stuck, uncertain which way to proceed because one does not have the materials, or the old process is not working. Suddenly, a different product or a different procedure comes to mind.

All three of these thinking skills come out of a mind that is versed in complexity and diversity and one that pushes, pulls, and stretches into brand new arenas.

Link to Richness

Creating, innovating, and inventing evolve from mixing together many pieces of information, concepts, and approaches until something new emerges. In some ways, this is close to the thinking skills of problem solving. The more complex the "thinking soup" becomes, the richer the possibilities for something new to appear. The more comfortable one is with diversity of ideas, the more possible innovative solutions become. Creating, innovating, and inventing expand the richness of thought and experience.

> **The more comfortable one is with diversity of ideas, the more possible innovative solutions become.**

Teaching Hints

To foster innovative and inventive thinking, teachers need to remember that different approaches work for different minds. For example, some students benefit from hearing certain kinds of music; some are helped by physical movement or physical exercise; and others will want to talk a bit to others before settling down to create something. Behaviors that look as if they are off-task behaviors may very well be creativity-enhancing behaviors. Helping students to identify what aids their creative thinking can help produce unexpectedly fine creative products.

Questions

Questions that address creativity, innovation, and invention sometimes are metaphorical in nature because metaphors will allow the mind to connect disparate items by imposing a shared similarity. Questions that encourage students to think "outside the box" are most useful here. Questions that foster creating, innovating, and inventing might include the following:

If all you had was x, y, and z, how could you create a, b, and c?

Besides depending on foreign oil or drilling in protected wilderness areas for domestic oil, what other ways would solve the energy crisis?

What metaphor can you use to explain this idea to someone else?

What would be an alternative way to get this result?

What are six possible solutions to this concern?

Using these five criteria or parameters, what are three possible architectural house plans that would meet them?

Graphic Organizer

The light bulb graphic organizer (Figure 2.4) is one way to help students lay out a variety of potential possibilities from which to choose the most innovative or helpful solution. In the light bulb, summarize the problem, the issues, or the parameters. Then, write possible solutions or methods on the spokes from the light bulb. In this brainstorming phase, it is not necessary to critique or throw out any of the ideas. Later, one can go back and either pick the best solution or method or combine some of these to create the best way to go.

■ □ ■ □ ■

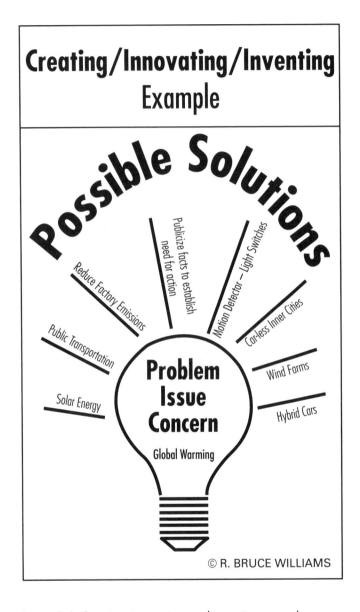

Figure 2.4. Creating, innovating, and inventing example.

RELATEDNESS

On a couple of recent business trips to the island city-nation of Singapore, I have noted some things that seem to work there. Singaporeans are quite a mixture of ethnic backgrounds. Chinese, Indians, Malaysians, and Westerners have learned to coexist in this populous modern city-nation. There are inevitable clashes from time to time, of course. However, on the whole, one is struck by the fact that basically this city-nation has discovered a secret in enabling diverse populations to live and work together. One simple tool that has been used is making sure that every housing area and every high rise apartment building has a mixture of ethnic backgrounds. This enables people personally to get to know others of different backgrounds. Transformation of thinking has allowed people to relate to each other in a way that works well in Singapore.

About Relatedness

One of the key functions of higher order thinking is to help the mind build connections among the myriad pieces of data it has absorbed and is absorbing.

It goes without saying that the quality of higher order thinking can have a huge influence on the quality of the experience of relatedness. The more whole and healthier the higher order thinking, the more whole and healthier the experience of relatedness. "The brain is a social brain" and "The search for meaning occurs through 'patterning'" are pertinent principles from Caine and Caine (1997, p. 19). Sylwester reminds educators: "Everything is connected to everything else" (1995, p. 140). The brain thrives on discerning and making connections. The more facile the higher order thinking, the more connections the brain can make and the more learning can occur. Indeed, the argument can be made that relatedness is the real function of all education.

The brain thrives on discerning and making connections.

BRIDGES AND CONNECTIONS

Without the capacity to see connections or to grasp relatedness, human beings would remain isolated and show stunted growth. Grasping relatedness may come naturally for some, while for others, it may need to be nurtured intentionally, even overcoming experiences that may have forced a defensive isolation. Sylwester says: "Our task as educators, however, is to help students begin to find *relationships* between the somewhat random, often trivial fact-filled experiences of everyday life and the fewer enduring principles that define life—and then to help them create and constantly test the memory networks that solidify those relationships" (1995, p. 103).

To fostering relatedness, teachers need to focus on thinking processes that encourage relatedness. This is why mere drill or fact memorization is not enough, particularly in a world of increasing diversity, global views, and especially in a work world depending more and more on men and women who can work well in teams. Relatedness

Mere drill or fact memorization is not enough.

■ □ ■ □ ■

includes the ability to relate to oneself, to others, and to the world around us. Like a three-legged stool, the capacity to relate to all three is crucial in becoming a highly functional adult in this century.

CHANGING RELATIONSHIPS

Higher order thinking helps students delve deeply into their relationships with self, others, and the world. Higher order thinking enables people to grow in their way of relating to self, others, and the world, and at times even to change their relationships to all three. Without this possibility, an abused child, who once learned to hate himself, would never be able to move toward accepting and loving himself. Without this possibility, men and women in a conflict could never move to any kind of reconciliation. Without this possibility, whole peoples or whole nations could never move away from hatred and hostility into living peacefully side by side.

Moving into higher order thinking means going beyond mere absorption of facts into the real concerns and issues of relatedness. These very life concerns and life issues can spark the higher order thinking teachers so want in students. "It is true that memorization can be quite complex. For example, we could learn how to 'analyze the causes of war' and then write in substantial detail about the differences between the Vietnam War and the Gulf War. However, even this type of knowledge tends to be surface knowledge; it does not prepare a student to solve complex problems and apply the knowlege to the unexpected and complex real-life situations" (Caine & Caine, 1994, p. 47).

Life concerns and life issues can spark the higher order thinking teachers so want in students.

■ □ ■ □ ■

THEMES AND TRENDS

When applied to one's relationship to self, others, and the world, higher order thinking helps people to step back far enough to see the themes and trends going on. Without higher order thinking, the self moves from one immediate moment to the next, from one instant gratification to the next. Without higher order thinking, relationships with others evolve into self-serving demands from others. Without higher order thinking, the world looks too complex, and one retreats into narrow communities or prejudiced, simplistic viewpoints. Goleman says it well: "Just one cognitive ability distinguished star performers from average: pattern recognition, the 'big-picture' thinking that allows leaders to pick out the meaningful trends from the welter of information around them and to think strategically far into the future" (1998, p. 33).

THE LIFE QUESTIONS

The key life questions for relatedness are quite straightforward: "How does anything I am studying or working on impact my relationships? What difference will any of this make to how I connect with myself, with others, and with the world? How does this give me clues about how I relate to myself, to others, and to the world? How will any of what I am studying or working on help me relate better to myself, others, and the world?" Unless educators make clear how higher order thinking influences these questions of relatedness, students may not see any reason to develop depth thinking skills.

Understanding Information — Skill of Connecting

Description of Strategy

The thinking skill of connecting is fundamental to seeing and feeling relationships. The capacity to discern connections is the capacity to relate pieces of information, feelings, concepts, life experiences, human customs, national interests, and so forth. Discerning connections requires an ability to step back far enough so that the associations become visible.

Link to Relatedness

Without the ability to connect, the mind is not able to perceive relatedness. In other words, the thinking skill of connecting is foundational for the whole process of experiencing relatedness. This goes far beyond connecting fact to fact or connecting idea to idea. This also involves discerning connections within one's own life and grasping themes or personality traits in one's personal life history. Furthermore, relatedness involves being able to make connections between self and another. Without the ability to relate, one lives in complete isolation. Finally, relatedness involves one group of people being able to make connections with what appears on the surface to be a very different group of people. To relate means that even hostile nations need to step back far enough to begin to make connections on a national level.

> **The thinking skill of connecting is foundational for the whole process of experiencing relatedness.**

Teaching Hints

One of the ways connecting has been promoted in the classroom is by linking new pieces of information to what a student has already learned previously. This strengthens the learning because the brain thrives on connections, patterns, and relationships.

> **The brain thrives on connections, patterns, and relationships.**

Questions

Questions and prompts that focus on connecting usually look for ways to express a relationship—similarity, bond, cause, affiliation, or link. Questions and prompts that foster connecting might look like the following:

> How is a particular character in the novel similar to you?
>
> How would you go about striking up a conversation with this character?
>
> How is it that the Russian nation today is relating in a comparatively friendly manner to the United States whereas thirty years ago the relationship was quite hostile?
>
> When have we encountered this theme before?
>
> When have you been surprised at a relationship that emerged where you least expected it? How did that happen?
>
> In your team of four, find five things you have in common.

Graphic Organizer

A graphic organizer very popular for discerning what students already know and what they want to learn is the KWL, created by Donna Ogle (1986; see Figure 3.1).

Using a KWL is very simple. When introducing a unit or lesson topic, begin by asking the students what they already know about the topic. After getting a list up in the K column, ask what they would like to learn about the topic. That list goes under the W column. Then, of course, at the end of the unit or the lesson, ask what they have learned and list that under the L column. This technique capitalizes on the brain research that reveals the importance for learning and memory of connecting new material to old. Also, by letting the students articulate their own questions, the teacher gets some level of interest and buy-in to the upcoming lesson or topic.

Although the KWL is a very powerful graphic organizer, obviously a teacher cannot use it all the time or the students will be bored. Variations include doing the three parts as a short conversation with no writing. Or, the teacher could create a different visual with the same questions. For example, I have often used a Web graphic organizer to organize what is already known.

After the KWL graphic has been created, display it in the classroom throughout the unit or topic. Threading content material through what the students wanted to learn communicates that their questions were taken seriously. Some teachers may want to go as far as building their whole content delivery around the questions the students asked. Other teachers may want to have student groups research the answers to the questions the students raised.

■ □ ■ □ ■

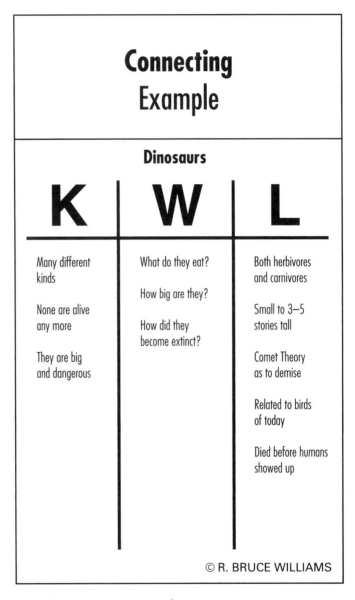

Figure 3.1. Connecting example.

Generating Insight—
Skill of Forcing Relationships

Description of Strategy

The thinking skill of forcing relationships comes about by attempting to find a connection between two things—ideas or sets of facts—that may at first appear to be very contradictory to each other. Studying these two contradictory items and working hard to see a relationship can sometimes call forth some very creative higher order thinking and display a unique and insightful connection that was not at all apparent originally. One image for this is those multicolored pictures that one needs to stare at for a while before one could see the hidden picture.

Link to Relatedness

It is one thing to see obvious or apparent relationships; it is quite another to be able to build a connection that was not obvious or create one in a situation that seemed to have blatant contradictions or disconnections. This calls for thoughtfulness that leads to unique insight as to what a connection might be. Forcing relationships calls for deep wrestling with the elements of the situation in order to wrest the connection out of the disconnection. The involvement here is much more intense and, unsurprisingly, much more rewarding.

Teaching Hints

The thinking skill of forcing relationships is a great way to bless tangential thinking. Very often in a class discussion a student will come out with what seems to be a totally off-the-wall, irrelevant comment. Rather than ignoring the student or chiding the student for not staying on the topic, teachers might ask the student how that student perceives the relationship. Posing such a question might call forth some very original and creative thinking. The more this is done, the more the class is encouraged into the realms of this kind of innovative thinking.

> **The thinking skill of forcing relationships is a great way to bless tangential thinking.**

Questions

Questions that help students with forcing relationships are those that ask students to focus on the similarities rather than the differences in two objects or situations. Questions that foster forcing relationships might look like this:

What is a way these two contradictory ideas might be similar?

How might these two antagonistic characters find a way to relate?

What are some possible scenarios that might lead to some resolution of the Middle East crisis?

What is the relationship you see between that comment you just made and the topic we have been talking about?

How might Shakespeare's *Hamlet* be espousing the same theme as the *Star Wars* sagas?

How does x remind you of y?

Was today's lesson more like a bowl of spaghetti or a dish of ice cream? Why?

Graphic Organizer

The right angle thinking graphic organizer (Figure 3.2) helps to encourage the thinking skill of forcing relationships. In the upper arrow, write the topic to be discussed. In the upper right, list the things that come to mind relative to that topic. When anything unusual or off target is suggested, add that to the list at the bottom left. When both lists are complete, find a name for the list at the bottom left and write that name in the lower arrow. Finally look at both lists and write a sentence that communicates the relationship between the two lists.

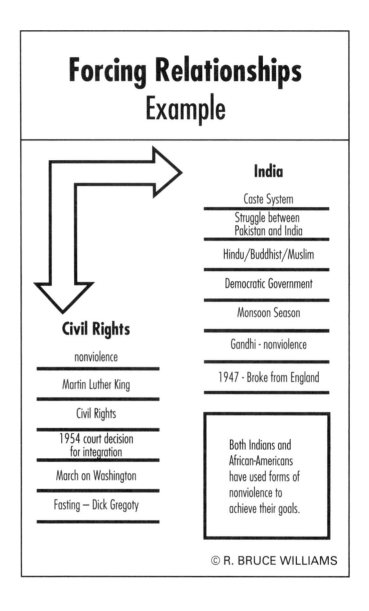

Figure 3.2. Forcing relationships example.

Discerning Implications—
Skill of Generalizing

Description of Strategy

The higher order thinking skill of generalizing pulls principles, ideas, themes, and values out of one situation and discerns how they are relevant in another situation. Generalizing is a kind of transfer very similar to Perkins' concept of low road transfer: "Low road transfer occurs when perceptual similarities of one situation to another trigger the making of a connection" (1995, p. 225). This kind of generalizing is most apt to occur in real-life situations, far from book learning. Generalizing in real-life situations is different than sitting back in the chair at your desk and pondering some interesting ideas. This kind of generalizing has to do with taking what has been learned in one situation or one life experience and relating that learning to another life situation.

Link to Relatedness

Generalizing is the test that says the learning has really been internalized. It is proof, so to speak, that the skill of relatedness has really become a part of one's higher order thinking. Generalizing is able to take specific ideas, values, and principles from one situation and relate them to another situation. It may mean taking a method learned in one class and using it in another class. It may mean culling out the learning from one life experience and using it in another life experience.

Teaching Hints

When beginning to teach generalizing, choosing very true-to-life situations to be compared for both the real-world and personal situations is crucial. For example, when using Figure 3.3, a graphic organizer (discussed in the Graphic Organizer section) that supports generalizing, this means using realistic, student-centered situations for both Situation One and Situation Two, which, in turn, requires that teachers know something about the lives of their students. Gradually, the teacher might move to a world situation derived from a story, an historical event, or a current event but might keep the personal situation very relevant to the students' lives. Down the line it might become possible to generalize from one abstract situation to another. As this is at the most difficult level in relatedness, this skill might take a lot of practice before the students are comfortable with it.

Questions

Generalizing is a vital life skill that requires a depth in reflective thinking that needs to be practiced and cultivated. Questions to ask that foster generalizing might sound like this:

Generalizing is a vital life skill that requires a depth in reflective thinking that needs to be practiced and cultivated.

What did this experience teach you?

How might this experience help you outside of class?

How did an experience of yours in the past help you figure out what to do here?

■ □ ■ □ ■

What was the breakthrough in the thinking about this situation that helped you figure out what to do here?

What was the principle, value, or idea that this character carried into this part of the story?

Given that this is what you really believe, what might you do differently next time this happens to you?

Graphic Organizer

The graphic organizer in Figure 3.3 is a simple tool to help students in the generalizing process. Begin by asking students to write some details about one situation in the triangle labeled Situation One. Then, have them jot down some details about another, new situation in the triangle labeled Situation Two. Have students study the details of Situation One, begin to pull out facts, principles, values, ideas, or perspectives, and write these details around the Situation One triangle. Move to the Situation Two triangle, and ask students to examine the details, and look for possible relationships between the principles, values, and ideas of Situation One and Situation Two.

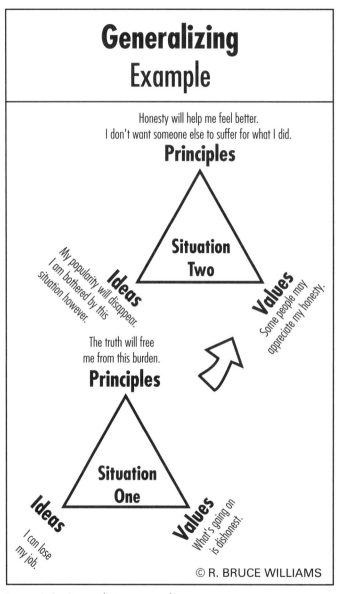

Figure 3.3. Generalizing example.

RIGOR

I heard a story once about a high school that decided to make its gifted program open and voluntary for anyone in the school. The story goes that several "C-level" students signed up for this program. There was a great deal of concern that these students, considered unprepared and probably unable to do the gifted class work, would be swamped and overwhelmed in the program. Shocking the educators, these students began to make As and Bs. Something about the challenge pushed their thinking capacities to higher levels.

About Rigor

Some clues that point to what rigor in thinking is all about come from noting certain student behaviors. For example, "Students demonstrate their risk-taking ability as they gain security in brainstorming, offering novel relationships, sharing original thoughts, tackling new problems, and requesting *not* to be given an answer because they want to figure it out for themselves" (Costa, 1991, p. 28). Students accustomed to rigorous thinking seek out new ways to use and test this rigor. The real test of rigorous thinking does not come when a student knows what to do to solve a problem. For Costa, the real test comes in how a student thinks comes when the student doesn't know what to do (1991, p. 9).

> **Students accustomed to rigorous thinking seek out new ways to use and test this rigor.**

Rigor leads to a crucial concept: "On my educational landscape, questions are more important than answers; . . . ." (Gardner, 1999, p. 24). An environment with many complex, relevant questions can bring about rigor in thinking. To accomplish this, teachers need to really think through instruction ahead of time.

Gardner (1999) adds other clues to what might be involved in rigor in thinking: "Metacognition, self-consciousness, intrapersonal intelligence, second-order thinking, planning (and revising and reflecting), systemic thinking, and their interrelations" (p. 52) all give us some sense of the flexible, curious, disciplined mind that displays rigor in thinking. As daunting as this all is, this kind of deep thinking is what school is about. Costa says, "Some students may perceive thinking as hard work, and therefore recoil from situations which demand 'too much' of it. Students, teachers, and administrators realize that learning to use and continually refine their intelligence behavior is the purpose of their education" (1991, p. 152). Rigor in thinking does not come by memorizing a lot of material, as important as certain content material is. Rigor in thinking comes by exercising the mind in thought-provoking problems and issues.

Caine and Caine (1997) suggest three elements that relate well to rigorous thinking. They refer to complex experience, relaxed alertness, and active processing (p. 178). When these three come together, rigorous thinking emerges.

COMPLEX LEARNING EXPERIENCES

It is fairly obvious that rigorous thinking cannot possibly come through learning tasks that are relatively simple to think through. If one is training for a 26-mile marathon, one doesn't stick to one-mile practice runs. Gradually, one needs to work up to the marathon length by running longer and longer distances. "Whereas short lectures and memorization play a part, much more learning takes place when learners are constantly immersed in complex experience; when they process, analyze, and examine this experience for meaning and understanding; and when they constantly relate what they have learned to their own central purposes" (Caine & Caine, 1997, pp. 18–19).

Achieving constant immersion in complexity is why such curricular approaches as problem-based learning and project work can contribute so much to the learning experience. Both instructional techniques involve a number of tasks, call upon a variety of intelligences, and require significant content learning to be completed well—well meaning that learning has been absorbed, understood, and then represented in more than just verbal ways. Teachers shortchange their students when they believe that they must always simplify learning tasks.

> **Teachers shortchange their students when they believe that they must always simplify learning tasks.**

Complex experiences within a discipline need to immerse students not only in significant content but also need to help students move toward thinking in that discipline's way of thinking. When teachers do this, they offer a much broader context for learning than just memorizing facts. Elder and Paul describe it like this:

> Content is not fragmented bits and pieces of information (which is the underlying assumption in didactic teaching) but a system with a definite set of logical relationships; and organized structure of

■ □ ■ □ ■

concepts, principles, and understanding; a system that requires the asking and answering of a certain set of questions and problems; and, ultimately, a disciplined mode of thinking. When one learns 'history,' for example, one learns to think historically. When one learns 'biology,' one learns to think biologically. When one learns 'anthropology,' one learns to think anthropologically. (1994, p. 34)

Rigor in thinking means being able to think as a discipline has taught one to think. Obviously, inculcating discipline-appropriate thinking patterns adds a radical change in how teachers teach the content in their classes. This goal suggests that "Content is selected because of its contribution to process and thus becomes a vehicle for thinking processes" (Costa, 1991, p. 7).

ENVIRONMENTS OF HIGH CHALLENGE AND LOW THREAT

Rigorous thinking is hampered in environments of high threat. Such high threat situations result in downshifting, defined by Caine and Caine:

We have defined *downshifting* as a psychophysiological response to threat associated with helplessness or fatigue (1994a). Downshifting inevitably results in less sophisticated use of the brain and a reversion to behaviors and patterns that have been previously "programmed." . . .That is, downshifting can foster memorization but interferes with higher-order and critical thinking and with creativity. (1997, p. 41)

■ □ ■ □ ■

In downshifting, the body and mind's attention is focused on how to reduce the apparent threat, leaving very little of the mind to engage in rigorous higher order thinking. As mentioned previously, a low challenge environment cannot foster rigorous thinking.

Caine and Caine propose an environment of "relaxed alertness" to overcome downshifting (1991, p. 134). "To maximize learning, we need to establish an environment that allows for safe risk taking. In essence, we need to eliminate pervasive or continuous threat. That sense of safety that welcomes appropriate risks is one part of what we mean by relaxation" (p. 132). Without this state of relaxation, a student cannot move into the challenge of high-level learning. Caine and Caine describe relaxed alertness: "There is an optimal state of mind for expanding natural knowledge. It combines the moderate to high challenge that is built into intrinsic motivation with low threat and a pervasive sense of well-being. We call that a state of 'relaxed alertness'" (p. 134). In other words, learners need some discomfort or some challenge to motivate the thinking process. It is only when the discomfort moves to threat that the thinking processes are hampered: "Relaxed alertness is *not* the same as being calm and unchanging. Although ongoing, it is a dynamic state that is compatible with a great deal of change" (p. 134).

A lot of factors contribute to the state of relaxed alertness. In addition to the classroom and the teacher, the whole school atmosphere and the outside community contribute to this state (Caine & Caine., 1991, p. 136).

It is a skillful teacher who can determine where that balance between high challenge and low threat lies with each student. Without that balance, rigorous thinking is difficult to achieve.

ACTIVE PROCESSING AND MULTIPLE REPRESENTATIONS

Although both complex experience and relaxed alertness are crucial, these alone are not enough. Caine and Caine identify the factor that is missing:

> Complex experience and relaxed alertness are critical; but if we want learning to improve significantly, then we have to help students capitalize on experience. Merely having a complex experience does not guarantee that much will be learned from it. The embedded ideas and skills must be brought to the surface, articulated, and demonstrated. (1997, p. 178)

Unprocessed material is not added to long-term memory. Reflective practices such as higher order questioning, journal writing, and group processing are needed if rigorous thinking is finally to become beneficial. Yet, "active processing is perhaps the most challenging aspect of brain-based learning" (Caine & Caine, 1997, pp. 178–179). Although teachers may implement complex experiences and create atmospheres of relaxed alertness, it often seems too time consuming to engage the students in active, reflective processing. Yet, it is only during active processing that includes multiple representations of content that everything comes together. It is only during this time that students finally experience the benefits of their concentrated efforts at rigorous thinking.

it is only during active processing that includes multiple representations of content that everything comes together.

■ □ ■ □ ■

THE LIFE QUESTIONS

Key life questions involving rigor include these:

> How is this material or how is this task worth my energy, my effort, and my thought?

> How can I experience the benefit of pouring my energy, effort, and thinking into this task, into this learning experience?

> How is the disciplined required going to be worth it?

The energy and thinking capacity are present in most students. The potential for rigorous thinking is there. When students will expend the necessary energy, effort, and thinking and can connect the learning experience with their personal experiences, then rigorous thinking comes naturally to them.

Understanding Information— Skill of Explaining Why

Description of Strategy

The thinking skill of explaining why is an entry point into rigorous thinking. This requires looking beneath, behind, and around material to discern what is not immediately apparent. This is related to cause-and-effect thinking and entails examining the effects thoroughly enough so that one can trace the effects back to some cause. The why's discerned during this examination cannot just be drawn from one's imagination, but must have some objective substantiation from the situation and material examined.

Link to Rigor

The discipline required to bring known facts together to discern the why beneath the surface is the link that connects explaining why to rigor. Sloppy thinking cannot reach sound conclusions about cause. Furthermore, relying on someone else's conclusions does not foster rigor. Explaining why requires learners to focus on what is known in order for them to become aware of the why's.

Teaching Hints

The act of explaining why gives the teacher ample opportunity to ask metacognitive questions about the student's process in coming up with answers of why. If the student's why is very off base, perhaps the metacognitive questions can reveal where in the thinking process the student went awry. Again, it is crucial to remember complex learning experiences, relaxed alertness, and active processing during these activities. Constant examination of these three can produce the kind of learning environment that supports this element of rigorous thinking.

Questions

Questions and prompts that help students explain why focus on reviewing the presented material and drawing logical, supported inferences from it. Questions and prompts that foster explaining why might be the following:

What information led you to this conclusion?

What other reasons could have produced these results?

Which explanation of why most closely links with the known information?

How could you test the accuracy of your analysis?

Given the known facts you have pulled together, what is your best guess as to what is going to be the result of these facts? (In other words, what might be the future results if we named these as why's?)

Give three reasons why the results of your experiment turned out differently from your hypothesis.

Graphic Organizer

The graphic organizer in Figure 4.1 simply puts the known facts before the student. By seeing these facts so clearly and perhaps by perceiving relationships not so apparent when the facts were not laid out on the organizer, the student may bring a sound grasp of the why to the surface. This organizer requires judgment as to which facts are really pertinent to the situation.

■ ☐ ■ ☐ ■

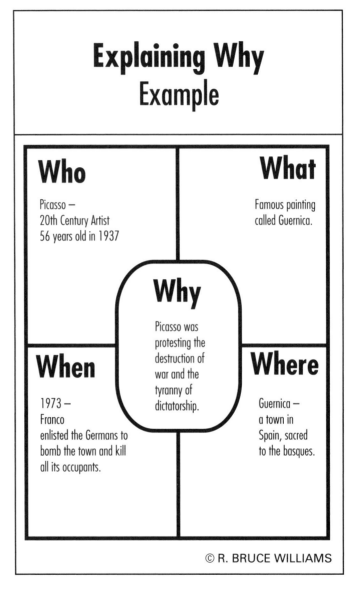

Figure 4.1. Explaining why example.

Generating Insight— Skill of Inferring

Description of Strategy

The thinking skill of *inferring* refers to the ability to read between the lines. When inferring, students look at the available data and make reasonable judgments about what has not been said directly. It is a bit like putting a puzzle together. When most of it is done, one knows what the picture is going to be even if all of the pieces are not in place yet. The difficulty in inferring is the skill's almost total reliance on the verbal/linguistic intelligence to find the clues to bring prior knowledge into play. The more the student can visualize what the words are communicating, the better the student can infer.

> **The more the student can visualize what the words are communicating, the better the student can infer.**

Link to Rigor

Only when students concentrate and focus their thinking can they create a picture of what is known and then make "educated" guesses about what is not known. As mentioned in the discussion of the explaining-why thinking skill, inferring is not making wild guesses that have no connection to what is known. Inferring is making sound discernments given the information available. This is its connection with rigor. Choosing the relevant facts from among all the known facts and then working with them to discern what is not directly known takes disciplined, rigorous thinking.

■ □ ■ □ ■

Teaching Hints

Although many students have difficulty in school when asked to exercise the formal skill of inferring, students make inferences all the time in their daily lives. For example, a girl sees her boyfriend talking to another girl. Right away, the girl assumes the boyfriend does not care about her anymore; she infers this conclusion, correctly or incorrectly, from the observed situation, and, perhaps, previous experience with the boyfriend. Walking down a city block, a student sees a noisy group of students from a rival school up ahead. That student may think that it might be wise to change the route to a safer one; he infers this is the best choice based on the current factual situation and prior knowledge of disputes between attendees of the two schools. Helping students to analyze what goes into their everyday inferring processes may also help them to apply inferring to more academic material.

> **Students make inferences all the time in their daily lives.**

Questions

Inferring implies drawing conclusions from observations. It is important that students base those conclusions on the observations and that they apply their prior knowledge to the observations. The inference that results should flow not only from the direct observations but also from the indirect knowledge provided by the student's experiences. Prior knowledge needs to be contextually logical, reasonable, and appropriate to the situation in order to support a correct inference.

■ □ ■ □ ■

Questions that foster inferring might be the following:

Given that this senator has voted for these three bills, what do you think her position will be relative to _____?

If the character was here from 3:00 - 5:00 and there from 7:30 to 9:30, where was this character from 5:00 - 7:30?

Where do you think you might have lost your wallet?

If your good friend isn't home, where might he be?

If you are stuck in an unmoving traffic jam and suddenly hear lots of police and fire sirens, what do you think lies ahead?

If a huge frost hits Florida for a week during growing season, which items are apt to increase in price next year?

Graphic Organizer

The simple graphic organizer in Figure 4.2 helps students organize and make obvious available relevant data so that they can infer more clearly. It is built on the premise that inferring is reading between the lines. Students list any possible relevant information in the rectangular data boxes. Then, they list one inference in the oval inference boxes. When they see the available information displayed, students can begin to figure out what that direct information is communicating indirectly.

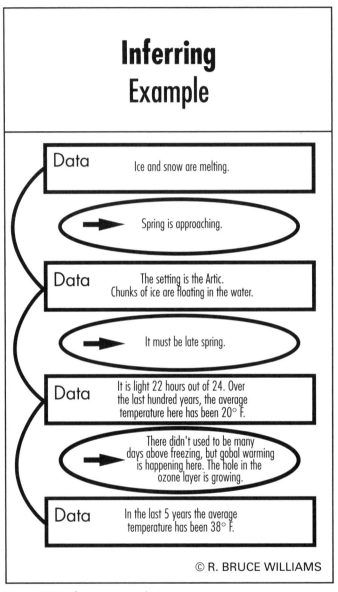

Figure 4.2. Inferring example.

Discerning Implications—Skills of Predicting and Sequencing

Description of Strategy

The thinking skill of *sequencing* is the skill of putting events, steps of instructions, or stages of mathematical or scientific processes in the proper order. It involves the ability to discern the bigger picture—where the events or steps of stages are going and how the pieces logically fit together.

The thinking skill of *predicting* goes one step beyond sequencing to look ahead into what has not yet happened and, based on the known status, to forecast what is going to happen or occur next. Both the skills of sequencing and predicting deal with ordering over time—past, present, or future.

> **Both the skills of sequencing and predicting deal with ordering over time—past, present, or future.**

Link to Rigor

It is this leap into the future unknown that makes this skill a part of rigorous thinking. Once again, when students are sequencing and predicting, they are not pulling their products out of thin air. They are creating sequences and predictions from known factual bases. Choosing what facts to work with requires focus. Choosing what options connect with the facts requires concentration.

It is this ability to sequence and predict that enables a person to discern the consequences of actions and decisions. It is no wonder that many people cannot see consequences clearly. It requires a very demanding and rigorous thinking. Often these are not emphasized in school.

Teaching Hints

Teachers need to let students become comfortable and familiar with the sequencing thinking skill before introducing predicting. Predicting based on reasonable leaps from available data is the most common skill needed in the classroom. Fantasy predicting (when predictions are not necessarily based on logic) is valid for some creative purposes.

Questions

Sequencing and predicting engage students in deeper thinking about a set of facts or a situation. Sequencing asks students to focus on discovering some kind of hierarchical, chronological, or causal relationship between given facts; predicting focuses their efforts on finding more logical facts that fit the relationship. Questions and prompts that foster sequencing and predicting might include the following:

> What are the six steps in correct order that will help someone solve this equation?
>
> List, step-by-step, what you will do to carry out this experiment.
>
> Given what you have read so far in the story, what do you think will happen next?
>
> Who do you think will win the election? What information has helped you to conclude that?
>
> What occurred before this story began?
>
> If the country goes to war, what will happen to the economy?

Graphic Organizer

The graphic organizer called bridging snapshots (Figure 4.3) is very appropriate for the sequencing and predicting thinking skills. This allows students to identify crucial scenes in a story or play, stages in a plant or animal development, steps to take in solving an equation, and so on. In addition, this organizer can be used for predicting. The large rectangle lists relevant facts to be ordered by some given criterion—time, alphabet, importance, or whatever; in the smaller rectangles, connected by arrows, students arrange those facts in order by the criterion. For practice predicting, the graphic provides more small rectangles than there are facts in the large rectangle, and students are asked to predict and visualize what, logically, would happen next. Some bridging snapshots might actually be pictures; others might be symbols, words, phrases, or sentences.

After bridging snapshot organizers have been created, displaying them in the room might be very helpful, particularly when the snapshots identify procedures or processes. When the graphic is available for students to consult, they might be able to internalize the procedures or processes more quickly. And, of course, the organizer also is useful for students' self-checking or for discovering what was left out or missed in performing the procedure or process.

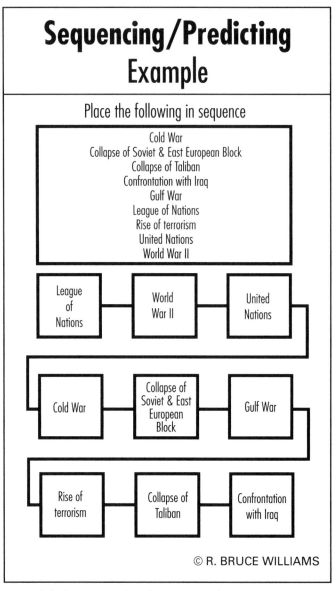

Figure 4.3. Sequencing/predicting example.

RECURSIVENESS

During high school, Lee demonstrated his mechanical aptitude and skill at working with his hands by opening a very informal electronic repair service for friends and family. A lot of people were amazed at his ability because he had had no formal training or study in electronics.

A few years later, Lee, very much at home with electronic machines, began working at Kinko's, home to many huge copiers capable of complex operations. He learned to deliver precisely what the customers wanted. To me, this represented a pretty simple transition from his electronic expertise to these huge machines.

However, now Lee is working for a biotechnology company that makes small intricate machines for use in the body. A lot of Lee's work is done through a microscope. He even uses a process called laser welding. This represents a huge leap from mechanical expertise into a vastly more complex and more risky line of work. Perkins's term (1995, p. 228) "high road transfer" might fit this transfer of Lee's electronic and mechanical ability into his new work world of biotechnology.

■ ☐ ■ ☐ ■

About Recursiveness

"Recursiveness guarantees transfer of learning. It is the difference between a single opportunity for concept/skill development, which is domain specific, and the transfer of learning across disciplines and across contexts in life. Learning is enhanced when it can be decontextualized and applied to new situations" (Fogarty, 1997, p. 58). *Recursiveness* has to do with the ability to extract meaning from one experience or event and see its effects or application to a completely different context.

Teachers frequently find diminished capacity for recursiveness in the classroom. "Teachers are often dismayed when they invite students to recall how they solved a similar problem and students don't remember, even though they've recently solved the same type of problem. They act as though they've never heard of it before. It's as if each experience is encapsulated into a separate episode that has no relationship to anything that came before or that comes afterward" (Costa, 1991, p. 26).

Costa's comment suggests that the capacity for recursiveness does not occur naturally in most students. In fact, research has borne out the fact that students do not generate recursiveness as often as teachers would like them to (Fogarty et. al, 1992, p. x). Recursiveness has to be taught very explicitly and patiently. Costa summarizes his hope in a change from viewing curriculum as a vehicle for learning content only to one utilizing the content and the discipline as a vehicle for teaching complex thinking skills, such as recursiveness:

> **Recursiveness has to be taught very explicitly and patiently.**

Rather than including science or math or the arts in the curriculum as ends in themselves, we will ask, what is the unique nature, structure, and modes of inquiry that can be drawn from each of these disciplines to be learned and applied elsewhere. As we make this fundamental shift, our instruction will be altered. We will change our view from learning *of* the content, to learning *from* the content. We will refocus from mastering content and concepts as an end, to the application of knowledge, the transference of cognitive strategies, and the tackling with confidence of new problems that command increasingly complex reasoning, more intricate logical and more imaginative and creative solutions. (Costa, 1991, pp. 164–165)

With expanding amounts of information, with rapidly changing careers and career tasks, recursiveness becomes more of a necessity for all students rather than a luxury for just the elite students.

LEARNING ACROSS SPACE AND TIME

Recursiveness makes learning real by applying it to many different contexts, both past experiences and future events. In this way, recursiveness helps students break the boundaries of space and time in learning—it becomes the ripple effect in learning.

Recursiveness highlights the usefulness of learning in many different contexts and in many different times, thus multiplying the benefit of that learning experience. When applied to a past context, usefulness may enable hidden meaning to emerge into consciousness. Or, when applied to the future, usefulness may occur years from the time of the learning. As Caine and Caine point out:

Therefore, something that is to be learned should not be restricted to an exercise in class, but should be meaningfully linked to as many areas of student lives as possible, including home, the broader world, friends and peers, and the whole school. . . .These other areas of our lives are where we find possible layers of experience, and the more we can engage them, the more real and vital the learning. (1997, p. 168)

Teachers find evidence of recursiveness from many different sources. Parents may mention different behaviors at home. Teachers may relate how a student applied a strategy learned in one content area to totally different content area (Costa, 1991, p. 27). Evidence of light bulbs lighting up in students' minds will be obvious.

Teachers find evidence of recursiveness from many different sources.

DELIBERATE DISCERNMENT

One of the secrets to recursiveness is its reliance on the student's ability to pull out a principle, a concept, or a theme from a learning, event, or personal experience. Without this step, no correlation appears between the original learning or experience and whatever is being encountered in the present. The situational details appear to be overwhelmingly different.

Perkins' distinction between low road (near) and high road (far) transfer is crucial to recursiveness: "Near transfer means applying the same knowledge or skill in very similar circumstances, whereas far transfer implies a big leap" (Perkins, 1995, p. 223). Near transfer seems more related to the thinking skill of generalizing talked about in regards to Relatedness. Perkins says, "[this kind of transfer is] pattern driven. It depends on abundant practice with the skill or knowledge in question, to set up the perceptual triggering. It is a phenomenon of experiential intelligence" (1995, p. 225).

As crucial a skill as this is, generalizing does not require the higher order thinking leap that recursiveness requires because recursiveness "depends on learners' deliberate mindful abstraction of principle" (Perkins, 1995, p. 226). There is not much to transfer with seemingly disconnected contexts unless one pulls out of the first context something general, which then can be used in another context:

> More thoughtful deliberate transfer tends not to occur unless the learning experience encourages students to be thoughtful—to seek generalizations, to look for opportunities to apply prior knowledge, to monitor their thinking, and ponder their strategies for approaching problems and tasks. Unfortunately, most instruction does not highlight this thoughtful side of learning. (Fogarty et. al, 1992, p. xvi)

Encouraging recursiveness calls for hard work on the part of the teacher, for it requires breaking down the process into smaller steps so that more and more students can make sense out of the process.

■ □ ■ □ ■

MOVING FROM ONE CONTEXT TO ANOTHER

Higher order thinking, as do many other endeavors, involves skill and practice. Recursiveness takes concentration and energy to accomplish the kind of transfer desired here. "Transfer will occur, given care to set up the conditions on which it thrives—the abundant diverse practice needed for low road transfer or the mindful abstraction needed for high road transfer"(Perkins, 1995, p. 228). Too often, teachers have not expected this high road transfer. Or, rather, teachers have expected it to occur naturally. It may occur naturally in some students; however, most students need explicit teaching of recursiveness, according to Perkins: "Finally, the argument from transfer warns that transfer is not to be taken for granted. Generality and widespread applicability of reflective intelligence do not occur automatically, . . . The bridging from one context to another has to be sought and prompted" (1995, p. 228). In an age where more and more higher order thinking skills are demanded in the workplace, teachers are often not taught directly about higher order thinking or how to teach higher order thinking skills. An additional challenge for teachers is to discover how recursive thinking is already going on in the lives of students.

> **Too often, teachers have not expected this high road transfer. Or, rather, teachers have expected it to occur naturally.**

THE LIFE QUESTIONS

Key life questions for recursive thinking help students apply knowledge to new situations. These life questions focus on the future: How is this valuable for my future? How will this learning or this event help me in the future? How will this learning or this event give me direction for my life and for my future? Recursive thinking helps one to imagine how an event or learning in one context can occasion concepts that will be beneficial in another totally different context. Recursiveness addresses direction, the future, and the big picture. Therefore, another life question could be: How may this learning or this event make a difference to my whole life?

In some ways, recursiveness may be the most difficult thinking skill area because of the focus by contemporary society on the "now." The most general desire in society is often "instant gratification." Recursiveness in thinking goes against both tendencies. An inability to project into the future may blind students to the value in the education they are receiving.

Understanding Information— Skill of Analyzing

Description of Strategy

The thinking skill of *analyzing* helps one to pull apart the subject being examined or helps one to garner learning, concepts, or themes from the subject. When analyzing, students need a viewpoint from which to see the parts or the emerging learning, concepts, or themes. This calls for the capacity to distinguish between big chunks and supporting details and to notice distinct themes and concepts running through several parts. These abilities to distinguish are crucial to grasping the significance of study material or life events.

Link to Recursiveness

Primary to recursive thinking is the ability to pick apart material to see what it is made of or what goes into it. Without this foundational understanding, students have nothing to transfer or project into the future to build recursive thinking. Building recursiveness depends not on details but rather on extrapolation from the details. It is the meaning and learning based on the details that relate and connect to other parts of the student's life or to the student's future.

Teaching Hints

Without some advance organizing by teachers, some students may not be able to master recursive thinking skills.

The thinking skills related to recursive thinking are not easily acquired for many students. It helps students learn when teachers can break down the process of analyzing into steps that make sense to students. Perhaps the teacher ends up with a series of questions or a progression of steps. Without some advance organizing by teachers, some students may not be able to master recursive thinking skills. Yet, these are the very skills that become more and more necessary as students, moving from job to job, are continually called on to figure out new concepts and new processes.

■ □ ■ □ ■

Questions

Analyzing requires "zooming out" in order to develop a broader view. Although details are the sturdy supports, analysis focuses on what those details are supporting. Questions that would foster analyzing might include the following:

What are the main elements of this idea?

What are the big pieces of this story? Of this act? Of this scene?

What are common themes running through this historical event?

When was the turning point of this story? When was the turning point of this war?

What are five basic reasons this happened? What details support your thinking here?

Where have you run into this concept or theme before?

Graphic Organizer

The concept map in Figure 5.1 is one appropriate graphic organizer to assist in the process of analyzing. In the center circle, write what the whole material or event is. Use the surrounding smaller circles to represent the parts or chunks of the material or sections of whatever event one is analyzing. Add the details that flesh out and explain what the smaller circles are about on spokes around the smaller circles. For many students, the visual aspect of this graphic facilitates their thinking about analyzing.

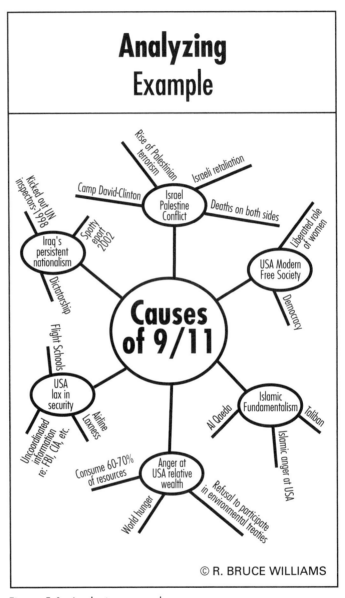

Figure 5.1. Analyzing example.

Generating Insight— Skill of Making Analogies

Description of Strategy

The thinking skill of making analogies is the skill of connecting a new concept, theme, or idea to something one is already familiar with. The precise connection may seem strange at first and may require further explanation of the actual connection. Ingenious analogies reveal a high level of thinking. Furthermore, this skill extends the process of analyzing. The more capable the analysis, the more thoughtful the analogy.

The more capable the analysis, the more thoughtful the analogy.

Link to Recursiveness

In one sense, the ability to make analogies is a test of how well one has understood the information one has just been analyzing. It is a step that helps students bridge the transfer into totally other contexts or into the their own futures. Making analogies forces learners to grapple with key insights and to translate these into something with which they are already familiar.

Teaching Hints

When working with this thinking skill, teachers need to dig beneath the stated analogy and expose the thinking process that helped the student to make the particular analogy. Creating analogies depends on relating known to unknown. Usually, an analogy highlights a quality or similarity between two things, using a quality from the known to shed light on the unknown.

Questions

It helps to ask explicit questions that enable the student to reveal the thinking used and the discovered connections. Questions that foster making analogies might be the following:

What does this remind you of?

How is this like what we were studying last week?

Why is _____ like _____?

How did you come up with that?

When have you felt this way before?

If you were to explain this to a younger student, how would you go about telling the student what this is like?

Graphic Organizer

The graphic organizer for making analogies shown in Figure 5.2 looks quite simple at first. On the left, one puts the concept, theme, or idea, while on the right, one puts what it is like. The crucial part is the "because" box under the two concept boxes. Here, students record their understanding of the relationship that the analogy is creating, thus displaying their insight into the process of making analogies. This box reveals students' understanding as well as their creative thinking.

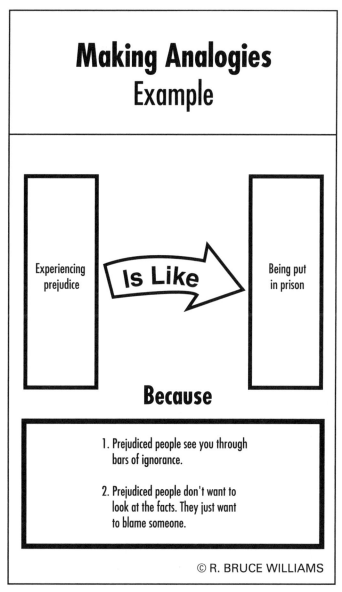

Figure 5.2. Making analogies example.

Discerning Implications— Skill of Transferring

Description of Strategy

The thinking skill of *transferring*, or what Perkins (1995) and Fogarty (1991) would call high road transferring, is the ultimate step of recursiveness. It is transfer that helps the student glean content or process from a science class and use the result in a history or geography class. Students are exercising transfer when they carry out at home or with peers a task they learned in school. Transfer enables a student to recall something learned years ago and apply it to a completely unique context in the learner's present life.

Link to Recursiveness

The capacity to discern applications in what might be less obvious contexts is precisely what recursive thinking is about. Recursiveness is fostered through the mind's ability to go wild in making connections. The more facile students become at transfer, the more they can display the benefits they derived from the learning or event.

Teaching Hints

Applying knowledge is a difficult thinking skill. Perkins acknowledges that "the track record of far transfer has not been good. A variety of investigations, initiated as far back as the turn of the century, has shown little far transfer from the study of intellectually rigorous subject matters"

(1995, p. 224). This situation levies demands on the guiding capabilities and the patience of teachers. Yet, by acquiring the skill to transfer, students potentially can ignite a deep desire to learn more and more. The benefit of learning finally sinks in. The important point is that students figure this out through their own higher order thinking.

> **By acquiring the skill to transfer, students potentially can ignite a deep desire to learn more and more.**

Questions

Transferring is one of the most important and primary goals of education. In spite of many efforts to foster transfer, it remains a difficult skill to teach and to learn. Questions and prompts that foster transferring might be the following:

How could what we learned today be useful for you if you were stranded on a desert island?

How could today's lesson help you if you found yourself in a land needing to speak a foreign language?

How could our lesson benefit you twenty years from now?

How might a musician make use of this mathematical concept?

How could our subject assist a space traveler centuries from now?

Describe how you discovered that today's lesson was useful to you at home.

■ □ ■ □ ■

Graphic Organizer

The graphic organizer for transfer is shown in Figure 5.3. First, describe the particular context or setting, using the outer ring of the Context One double circle. Then, use the inner circle to record the useful principles, concepts, or themes gleaned from that first context. Next, use the outer ring of the Context Two circle surrounding the square to describe the second context or setting. Finally, record within the square the way one or more of the gleaned principles, concepts, or themes illuminates or guides one in the second context. It does not matters whether these illuminations seem far-fetched or not, for they have come from the analysis and analogies in the first context.

■□■□■

Transferring
Example

Context One

Following the steps in a math process.

There are often steps. It's often easier to follow them.

Context Two

Putting a toy together.

Hooking up a computer.

Study the installation manual first.

© R. BRUCE WILLIAMS

Figure 5.3. Transferring example.

CONCLUSION

Although many teachers are overwhelmed at the thought of moving beyond helping students grasp just the factual material, others find that engaging students in higher order thinking enables their students to grasp and retain content with deeper understanding. The questions and graphic organizers presented for each level of thinking within each category of concern are geared to move students into critical questioning and higher order thinking.

The life questions try to demonstrate the day-to-day necessity of gaining competence with these skills. Enjoy the relevance, richness, relatedness, rigor, and recursiveness when they occur in your classroom!

Appendix A: Brainstorming and Planning Lessons

BRAINSTORMING QUESTIONS

Let's apply the thinking skills and organizers to an academic context. One way to do this is to choose an upcoming unit and to write questions using the five Rs. Figure A.1 might help the brainstorming process. Several sample questions are included to illustrate the possibilities of this chart.

QUESTION BRAINSTORM

© R. BRUCE WILLIAMS

RELEVANCE-CONTEM-PORANEITY	RICHNESS-COMPLEXITY	RELATEDNESS-CONNECTEDNESS	RIGOR-CHALLENGE	RECUR-SIVENESS-CONCEPT
What are the similarities and differences between x and y?	What are your criteria for deciding this is the most important?	Knowing what you already know, what do you now need to find out?	What drove this character to do this.	Determine five causes for this historical event!
What is your view of ____?	Describe a student's life fifty years from now?	What is the connection between x and y?	When you mixed this chemical with that chemical, why did it explode?	Where did this person make his mistake in his attempt to solve this?
How does that make you feel?	Given what you now know, create a picture of this character.	When you hear this, what does it make you think about?	Knowing this person's skills, what do you think her occupation is?	Feeling someone's prejudice toward you is like ____?
Which is the option you think is best?	How might we solve our land-fill problem?	Where else could you use this?	What is going to happen next in this play?	Ten years from now, how is this going to help you?
Why might we need to know this?				
How can you use this?				

Figure A.1. Brainstorming Questions

HIGHER ORDER THINKING SKILLS LESSON PLAN

Educators have discovered in the past two decades that higher order thinking skills do not appear automatically in most students. Some students do become cognizant of their various thinking skills and ways of thinking through their own inductive process. Other students need to be coached to discern what various thinking skills are, which ones they are good at, which ones they need to improve, and, finally, how to go about enriching and improving their thinking skills.

Educators believe that specific higher order thinking skills often need to be taught explicitly and directly at various points in a unit or during a semester. Figure A. 2 shows a completed planning form to guide the creation of a lesson that teaches a thinking skill explicitly.

HIGHER ORDER THINKING SKILL LESSON PLAN

Lesson Objective
To teach sorting and classifying

Hook
Play a contemporary popular song the students know. Ask what they think playing a song has to do with higher order thinking skills.

Instruction
Talk about the thinking skills of sorting and classifying. It will be helpful to use a T-Chart with one side being "What is it?" and the other side being "How does one do it?" Generate some responses on each side until it seems clear what it is and how one does it. Do one chart for sorting and one chart for classifying.

Practice
Give student teams either 20–25 popular music song titles or 20–25 names of singers or music groups. Ask each team to sort them into clusters however they see fit. Then ask the teams to label the clusters with their own category name.

Monitoring
Be sure to check in with each group to observe how they are doing. Help groups that might be stuck or might have questions. Mention later helpful dialogue or strategies you observed teams using to sort and classify.

Celebration
Have teams share their categories. Ask some of the following questions. What were some of the similarities you noticed? differences? What kinds of thinking and decisions went on to sort and classify. How is this thinking skill useful outside of school?

© R. BRUCE WILLIAMS

Figure A.2. Higher order thinking skill lesson plan.

Steps to use this lesson plan:

1. Lesson Objective: Name the specific thinking skill to be taught.

2. Hook: Decide how to get the students' attention and how to demonstrate the usefulness or helpfulness of the specific thinking skill.

3. Instruction: Decide how to teach the various aspects of the specific thinking skill and how to make the thinking skill visible so that the students know exactly what is being talked about (i.e., prepare some questions and decide which graphic organizer to use).

4. Practice: Decide what activity will help students to practice the thinking skill and whether this activity will be done individually, in pairs, or in larger groups.

5. Monitoring: Decide how to monitor and observe the specific thinking skill in practice. Consider if there are ways the peers in the group can monitor this. Plan time for the teacher to walk around and observe what is happening in order to sense how the students are learning and using the thinking skill.

6. Celebration: Finally, decide how to help students honor and celebrate their progress. For example, consider rewards such as reading a story, showing a short video, or giving students 10 minutes of free time to celebrate their learning.

Appendix B:
Blacklines of Graphic Organizers

The graphic organizer blackline masters are arranged in the same order as they were introduced in the text.

Appendix B figure number	Title of graphic organizer	Figure number in text
B.1	Comparing/Contrasting worksheet—Venn	1.2
B.2	Comparing/Contrasting worksheet—Y	1.3
B.3	Evaluating/Judging worksheet	1.4
B.4	Applying worksheet	1.5
B.5	Classifying/Sorting/ Ranking worksheet	2.1
B.6	Ranking worksheet— Ladder	2.2
B.7	Visualizing/Imagining worksheet	2.3
B.8	Creating/Innovating/ Inventing worksheet	2.4
B.9	Connecting worksheet	3.1
B.10	Forcing Relationships worksheet	3.2

■□■□■

Comparing/Contrasting
Worksheet

© R. BRUCE WILLIAMS

Comparing/Contrasting
Worksheet

© R. BRUCE WILLIAMS

Evaluating/Judging
Worksheet

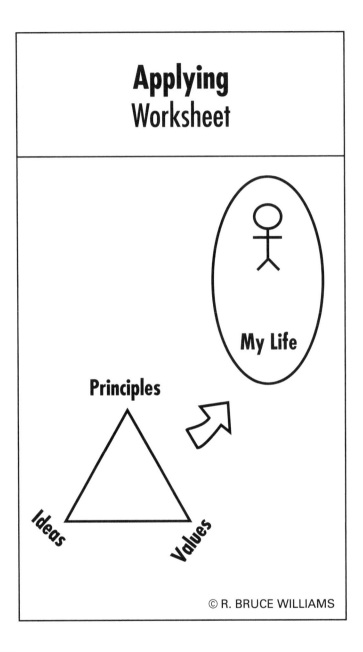

Classifying/Sorting/Ranking
Worksheet

© R. BRUCE WILLIAMS

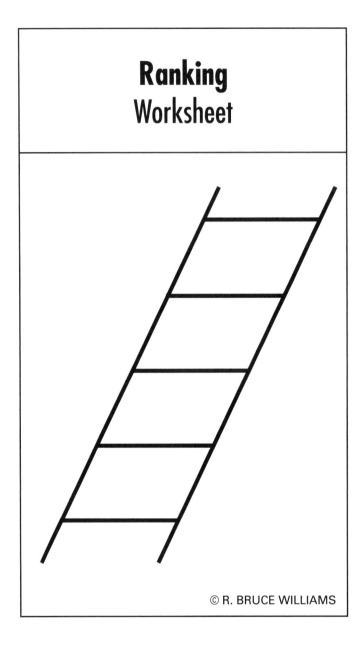

Ranking
Worksheet

© R. BRUCE WILLIAMS

Visualizing/Imagining
Worksheet

Looks Like	Sounds Like	Feels Like

© R. BRUCE WILLIAMS

Creating/Innovating/Inventing
Worksheet

Possible Solutions

**Problem
Issue
Concern**

© R. BRUCE WILLIAMS

Connecting
Worksheet

K	W	L

© R. BRUCE WILLIAMS

Forcing Relationships
Worksheet

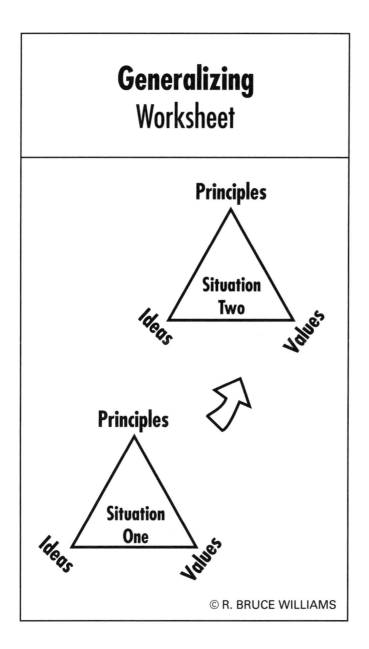

Generalizing
Worksheet

© R. BRUCE WILLIAMS

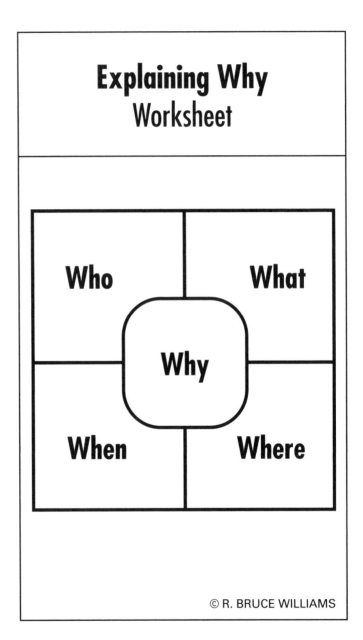

Inferring
Worksheet

Data

→

Data

→

Data

→

Data

© R. BRUCE WILLIAMS

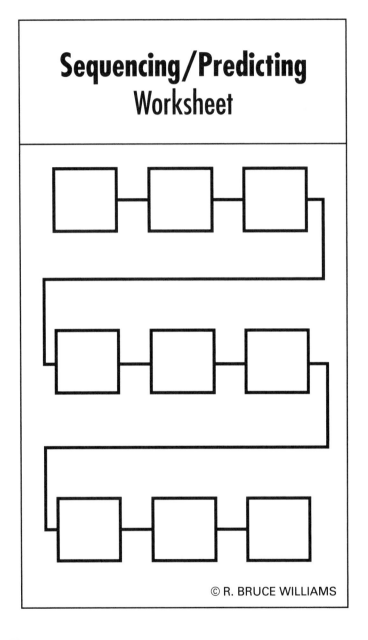

Analyzing
Worksheet

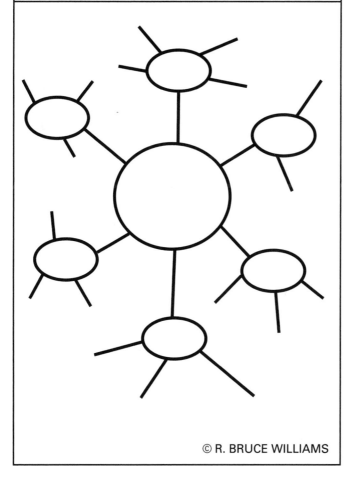

Making Analogies
Worksheet

Is Like

Because

© R. BRUCE WILLIAMS

Transferring
Worksheet

© R. BRUCE WILLIAMS

QUESTION BRAINSTORM

© R. BRUCE WILLIAMS

RELEVANCE- CONTEM- PORANEITY	RICHNESS- COMPLEXITY	RELATEDNESS- CONNECTEDNESS	RIGOR- CHALLENGE	RECUR- SIVENESS- CONCEPT

HIGHER ORDER THINKING SKILL LESSON PLAN

Lesson Objective	Hook
Instruction	
Practice	

Monitoring	Celebration
	© R. BRUCE WILLIAMS

BIBLIOGRAPHY

Bellanca, J. & Fogarty, R. (1986). *Catch them thinking: A handbook of classroom strategies.* Glenview, IL: Pearson SkyLight Professional Development.

Bellanca, J. & Fogarty, R. (1991). *Blueprints for thinking in the cooperative classroom.* Thousand Oaks, CA: Corwin.

Ben-Hur, M, (Ed.). (1994). *On Feuerstein's instrumental enrichment: A collection.* Glenview, IL: Pearson SkyLight Professional Development.

Black, S. (2001). Child or widget? *Journal of Staff Development, 22*(4), 10–13.

Caine, G., Caine, R. N., & Crowell, S. (1994). *Mindshifts: A brain-based process for restructuring schools and renewing education.* Tucson, AZ: Zephyr Press.

Caine, R. N., & Caine, G. (1991). *Making connections: Teaching and the human brain.* Alexandria, Virginia: Association for Supervision and Curriculum Development.

Caine, R. N., & Caine, G. (1997). *Education on the edge of possibility.* Alexandria, VA: Association for Supervision and Curriculum Development.

Costa, A. L. (1991). *The school as home for the mind.* Thousand Oaks, CA: Corwin.

Csikszentmihalyi, M. (1990). *Flow: The psychology of optimal experience.* New York: Harper & Row.

Doll, W. E. (1993). Curriculum possibilities in a 'post' future. *Journal of Curriculum and Supervision, 8*(4), 277–292.

Elder, L. & Paul, R. (1994). Critical thinking: Why we must transform our teaching. *Journal of Developmental Education, 18*(1), 34–35.

Elder, L. & Paul, R. (1997). Critical thinking: The key to emotional intelligence. *Journal of Developmental Education, 21*(1), 30–41.

Elder, L. & Paul, R. (1998). Critical thinking: Developing intellectual traits. *Journal of Developmental Education, 21*(3), 34–35.

Fogarty, R. (1990). *Designs for cooperative interactions.* Thousand Oaks, CA: Corwin.

Fogarty, R. (1994). *How to teach for metacognitive reflection.* Thousand Oaks, CA: Corwin.

Fogarty, R. (1995). *Best practices for the learner-centered classroom.* Glenview, IL: Pearson SkyLight Professional Development.

Fogarty, R. (1997). *Brain compatible classrooms.* Glenview, IL: Pearson SkyLight Professional Development.

Fogarty, R. (2002). *Brain compatible classrooms* (2nd ed.). Thousand Oaks, CA: Corwin.

Fogarty, R., & Bellanca, J. (1991). *Patterns for thinking patterns for transfer.* Glenview, IL: Pearson SkyLight Professional Development.

Fogarty, R., Perkins, D., & Barell, J. (1992). *How to teach for transfer.* Glenview, IL: Pearson SkyLight Professional Development.

Fusco, E. & Fountain, G. (1992). Reflective teacher, reflective learner. In A. Costa, J. Bellanca, & R. Fogarty (Eds.), *If minds matter: A foreword to the future: Vol. 1,* (pp.239–255). Arlington Heights, IL: SkyLight Publishing.

Gardner, H. (1983). *Frames of mind.* New York: Basic Books.

Gardner, H. (1999a). *The disciplined mind: What all students should understand.* New York: Simon and Schuster.

Gardner, H. (1999b). *Intelligence reframed.* New York: Basic Books.

Goleman, D. (1995). *Emotional intelligence.* New York: Bantam Books.

LeDoux, J. (1996). *The emotional brain.* New York: Touchstone.

Ogle, D. (1986). K-W-L group instruction strategy. In A. Palincsar, D. Ogle, B. Jones, & E Carr (Eds.), *Teaching techniques as thinking (Teleconference resource quide).* Alexandria, VA: Association for Supervision and Curriculum Development.

Parry, T. & Gregory, G. (1998). *Designing brain compatible learning.* Thousand Oaks, CA: Corwin.

Paul, R. (1993). *Critical thinking; What every person needs to survive in a rapidly changing world.* Dillon Beach, CA: The Foundation for Critical Thinking.

Paul, R. (1999). *Critical thinking; Basic theory and instructional strategies.* Dillon Beach, CA: The Foundation for Critical Thinking.

Perkins, D. (1995). *Outsmarting IQ: The emerging science of learnable intelligence.* New York: The Free Press.

Prenctice, M. (1994). *Catch them learning.* Thousand Oaks, CA: Corwin.

Schrenko, L. (1994). *Structuring a learner-centered school.* Thousand Oaks, CA: Corwin.

Silberman, M. (1996). *Active learning: 101 strategies to teach any subject.* Boston, MA: Allyn and Bacon.

Sylwester, R. (1995). *A celebration of neurons: An educator's guide to the human brain.* Alexandria, VA: Association for Supervision and Curriculum Development.

U.S. Department of Labor. (1992). *Learning a living: A blueprint for high performance: A scans report for America 2000.* Washington, DC: U.S. Government Printing Office.

Wheatley, M. J. (1992). *Leadership and the new science.* San Francisco: Berrett-Koehler Publishers.

Williams, R. B. (2002a). *Cooperative learning: A standard for high achievement.* Thousand Oaks, CA: Corwin.

Williams, R. B. (2002b). *Multiple intelligences for differentiated learning.* Thousand Oaks, CA: Corwin.

Williams, R. B. & Dunn, S. E. (2000). *Brain compatible learning for the block.* Thousand Oaks, CA: Corwin.

Wolfe, P. (2001). *Brain matters: Translating research into classroom practice.* Alexandria, VA: Association for Supervision and Curriculum Development

Zemelman, S., Daniels, H., & Hyde, A. (1993). *Best practice: New standards for teaching and learning in America's schools.* Portsmouth, NH: Heinemann.

Teachers Make ⋊ the Difference

The good teacher *instructs,*
    the excellent teacher *invites,*
        the superior teacher *involves,*
            the great teacher *inspires.*

Robin Fogarty—Chicago, 1999

CORWIN

A SAGE Company

The Corwin logo—a raven striding across an open book—represents the union of courage and learning. Corwin is committed to improving education for all learners by publishing books and other professional development resources for those serving the field of PreK–12 education. By providing practical, hands-on materials, Corwin continues to carry out the promise of its motto: **"Helping Educators Do Their Work Better."**